JALI

JALI

Lattice of Divine Light in Mughal Architecture

Navina Najat Haidar

With photography by **Abhinav Goswami**

Contributions by
Mitchell Abdul Karim Crites,
George Michell and **Ebba Koch**

MAPIN
PUBLISHING

Contents

FOREWORD

*J*alis bring together the aesthetics of the Indian subcontinent and the Islamic world. On our many explorations of Mughal architecture, my late husband Nasser Sabah al-Ahmad al-Sabah and I often stood in the dappled light and gentle breeze of a *jali* screen to appreciate the beauty of the buildings and the landscape beyond. Nasser had a true affinity for all things beautiful, and jewelled objects from the Mughal dynasty were a special passion of his. Like the jewels, *jali* screens play with light and display a similar sense of refinement. Like the jewels, these beautifully carved *jali* screens are part of a greater Mughal art. This volume, through its scholarly discussion and skilled photography, captures the importance of the *jali* in the story of Mughal life, architecture and related traditions.

The study of the *jali*, both within the context of Mughal architecture and ornament as well as independent of it, allows us to consider its full artistic, expressive and metaphorical potential. Under the gifted and knowledgeable eye of Dr Navina Najat Haidar, the Nasser Sabah al-Ahmad al-Sabah Curator-in-Charge of the Department of Islamic Art at the Metropolitan Museum of Art, this study of the *jali* allows us to better understand how all the pieces of a Mughal edifice fit together. Through her, we can discover the excellence of the Mughal-era craftsmen, workshops, architects and artisans.

Hussa Sabah al-Salem al-Sabah
Director General, Dar al-Athar al-Islamiyyah
Co-owner, The al-Sabah Collection

PREFACE

Set in window openings or as magnificent lofty walls, *jali*s (jālī, Hindi, network, net, lattice, trelliswork†) are carved and perforated screens in the architecture of south Asia. This volume on the *jali* began with conversations with Stuart Cary Welch in his 'Jali Mahal' in New Hampshire, and Mitchell Abdul Karim Crites in New Delhi, who both shared a common appreciation for this distinctive feature in Mughal buildings. Once embarking upon this study, it became clear that Mughal *jali*s had to be understood within the context of earlier traditions of stone carving in the subcontinent and wider exchanges with other parts of Asia and the Mediterranean. Thus, the scope expanded to include broader artistic styles, connections and philosophies that together gave rise to the powerful artistic language of the *jali*.

Following the Introduction, the chapters in this volume are organized chronologically, tracing the development of the Mughal and Sultanate *jali* through three principal design formats, namely, a) square grids enclosing auspicious symbols of ancient Indian form, mainly in the Gujarat Sultanate; b) geometric patterns relating to the idea of 'celestial mathematics' and allegories of divine light in early Mughal architecture; and c) floral trellises relating to a wider language of paradisiacal allusion in Shah Jahani gardens and buildings. Further inventive compositions in Rajput, Deccan and British-era buildings are discussed in the later chapters dedicated to these variations, while modern legacies of the *jali* are explored in the final section of the volume. Thematic contributions by George Michell, Ebba Koch and Mitchell Abdul Karim Crites are interspersed in the sequence of chapters.

Many *jali*s are now detached from their buildings, but effort has been made to show surviving *in situ* examples in order to contextualize them in their original settings. These include both familiar and lesser-known sites, many newly photographed for this book. The approach to the material relies on connoisseurship and an appreciation of style, and the text also explores the patrons and personalities associated with the sites. However, the *ustad*s, or masters, who created the *jali*s and other ornamental features in buildings remain largely anonymous, as do the majority of craftsmen of the Mughal age. This book aims to document, contextualize and celebrate the *jali*s of the Mughal world and their makers for both specialist and general readers.

---

†Platts, *A Dictionary of Urdu, Classical Hindi and English*, 372.

Introduction

"...that kind of glancing, slightly dematerialized quality of what one does actually see in reality..."

Howard Hodgkin, Ahmedabad, 1982[1]

As the first Islamic buildings of the late-seventh to early-eighth century in the eastern and western Mediterranean were beginning to establish new formulas of space, ornament and fenestration, distant India, as yet untouched by their influence, was also seeing important developments in its burgeoning styles of freestanding temple architecture. While cultures and inspirations profoundly differed, architects at both ends were simultaneously shaping light and views through pierced screens into the realm of the sacred space. We find remote echoes between the marble interlace windows in early mosques and the perforated stone screens of Indian temples, developing separately and locally. Each advanced the techniques, styles and understanding of materials for artisans. With the introduction of Islamic styles of architecture to India from the late twelfth century onwards, these traditions met and the pierced and carved *jali* screen came into a new visual vocabulary. Middle Eastern designs, which had expanded in scope over time, were interpreted and executed by Indian stone carvers experienced in the existing local styles. Like so much of Indo-Islamic architecture, *jali*s thus represent a marriage of traditions. Replete with symbolism, the Indian *jali* evolved to become both a technical and an aesthetic marvel in Mughal-period buildings, and eventually an international 'Islamicate' style of the modern age.

Celestial imagery in Mughal art exalted the power of the sun and the mysticism of the stars set in the heavenly sphere, which were evoked in the radiating sunbursts (*shamsa*s), stellar (*sitara*) shapes and geometric knot patterns (*girih*) of *jali* windows and screens. The motifs of divine illumination were integral to Sufism as were allegories of light in Islam, such as the Verse of Light where God is likened to a light from a lamp in a niche (*"God is the light of heavens and the earth. The symbol of His light is as a niche, wherein is a lamp..."*, Qur'an, 24.35).[2] In Mughal tombs, mosques and palaces, *jali*s mediated between heavenly light and the world of man through a sophisticated language of mathematical patterns, reflections and shadows.

The skilful techniques of carving *jali*s are a testament to the abilities of Indian stonecutters and craftsmen, who remain largely anonymous, and the tastes of discerning patrons and builders (see essay by MAK Crites). Materials used include sandstone, marble, basalt, stucco, wood and even iron. Mughal *jali*s appear light and airy, emerging from large blocks of stone with the use of stencils, drills, and small chisels (although the original techniques are not well understood). Their sheer size, since often designed to act as entire walls, transformed the appearance of buildings.[3] Such large *jali*s are often constructed from two or three separate pieces but almost seamlessly joined so as to appear as one continuous form. This monumentality can be seen in the marble screens that were made for the tomb of Sheikh Salim Chishti at Fatehpur Sikri and that of Itimad ud-Daula, probably by the same Agra workshop. In both these sites, the delicate marble screens, each over eight feet in height, create a filigree shroud that envelops the upper or lower structure of the building (see 'Divine Order', figs 18 and 21).

In terms of style, the Mughal *jali* evolved most immediately from precedents of the earlier Sultanate age. Sacred symbols and square-grid formats of *jali*s in shrines and mosques of Sultanate Gujarat themselves clearly display a debt to earlier Hindu and Jain temple traceries of the region (see 'Sacred Symbols' and essay by George Michell). *Jali*s of the Delhi Sultanate and central India on the other hand incorporated distinctive styles from the Islamic west, such as geometric star-and-hexagon patterns and arabesque scrollwork (see 'Celestial Geometry'). Early Mughal *jali*s in the buildings of Akbar and Jahangir combined these formulas with fresh inspiration and new materials. These *jali*s continued to stay true to the geometric patterns and stellate designs that had evolved in the wider Persianate world while also integrating auspicious Hindu and Jain motifs such as floral heads and swastika meanders (see 'Divine Order'). Mughal *jali*s in Shah Jahani buildings took off in another stylistic direction, abandoning celestial order for paradisiacal floral trellises of organic form (see 'Heavenly Gardens' and essay by Ebba Koch). Meanwhile, contemporary Deccan sultanates in the south had their own distinctive styles of architecture, featuring fantastical and calligraphic *jali* designs and dazzling geometry in carved stucco (see 'Fantasy and Formality'). Through the eighteenth and nineteenth centuries, the imperial Mughal style of cusped arches and floral screens became spectacularly elaborated at Rajput forts and palaces, especially in the secluded areas of courtly women (see '*Jali* Mania'). This '*jali* mania' evolved into further stylistic variations in the buildings of the British Raj and the 'Indo-Saracenic' style of monuments, such as the Gateway of India in Mumbai. Innovations of the *jali* within global architecture of the modern age and as a form of individual expression by contemporary artists continue to the present day (see '*Jali* in the Modern Age').

❖ The *Jali* Lamp

Before the electric age, the source of nightlight in all societies was a flame, fuelled by oil, coal or some other source and contained within a holder. These included hand-held oil lamps; lanterns; long candles in candlestands; open flames on poles or torches; and varieties of standing, resting or footed lamps. Some of these were enclosed within pierced walls to create a pattern that would be reflected outwards while also shaping the view of the internal light. These effects and experiments with light and pattern must have played a role in the development of aesthetics of pierced screens as visual analogues.

Terracotta or unglazed clay lanterns—the lamp of the simple villager all over the world—survive from the ancient world and are still widely produced today in rural and urban South Asia. Their shapes often echo an architectural form with the appearance of pierced walls, such as an example from Roman Egypt in the form of a wayside shrine with peaked roof and open crossbar walls (fig. 1). From Nishapur excavations, a good number of such unglazed lamps appear in whitish earthenware (fig. 2). The walls are pierced with a simple geometric grid, usually triangular openings, through which the light would have been thrown out. Glazed ceramic lamps with pierced openings are also known, such as a mosque lamp attributed to Raqqa, Syria, which displays stars and interlace openings on the sides (fig. 3).

FIG. 1
Roman terracotta lantern in the shape of a wayside shrine, Egypt, c. 2nd century
The Metropolitan Museum of Art, Gift of Joseph W. Drexel, 1889, 89.2.2092

FIG. 2
Earthenware lantern with pierced walls, Nishapur, Iran, 9th–10th century
The Metropolitan Museum of Art, Rogers Fund, 1939, 39.40.87

FIG. 1

FIG. 2

From excavations at Rayy, fragments of lamps cut from sheet metal display fine scrolling vegetal designs.[4] A complete mosque lamp of this type, now in the David Collection, Copenhagen, is attributed to tenth-century Iran or Iraq (fig. 4). Its sheet brass body displays an openwork pattern executed in a delicate web of rounded scale-like openings bearing bold Kufic inscriptions (the accompanying chain is probably of later date). An internal glass bowl would have held the wick and oil, throwing out dappled patterns.

The model of a pierced openwork mosque lamp continued through the later periods of Islamic history, some associated with royal patronage.[5] Impressively large ensembles of such lamps evolved, either as large single pieces almost resembling architectural edifices or assembled and hung together in a stacked circular installation below a dome, as was popular in Ottoman interiors. Sheet metal pierced mosque lamps were also favoured by British restorers for the interior of Mughal monuments. Lord Curzon's gift of a perforated Cairene 'Saracenic' lamp for the Taj Mahal cupola, for example, reflects the tracery of the marble screens all around. Any other choice might have seemed heavy for such an ethereal space.[6]

FIG. 3

FIG. 4

FIG. 3
Glazed earthenware mosque lamp with pierced walls and relief inscriptions, Raqqa, Syria, 13th century
The Metropolitan Museum of Art, Henry G. Leberthon Collection, Gift of Mr and Mrs A. Wallace Chauncey, 1957, 57.61.17

FIG. 4
Openwork, sheet brass mosque lamp with Qur'anic inscriptions, Iran or Iraq, 10th century
The David Collection, Copenhagen, Inv. No. 17/1970

❖ The Miniature *Jali*

While we think of *jali*s as primarily architectural, many Indian and Middle Eastern luxury wares and practical objects contain pierced designs resembling miniature *jali*s. These generally take the form of openwork geometric or vegetal interlace or pierced stars, medallions and floral heads, often sharing the same designs as large windows and screens. Around the world, from Spain to India, Muslim craftsmen came to be recognized for the community's ability to execute such fine and delicate work.

A Persian bronze plaque of the Seljuq period (fig. 5) displays scrolling arabesques and cartouches and its powerful thick lines recall, on a small scale, the aesthetics of an iron window *jali* of the sixteenth century in Bijapur (see 'Fantasy and Formality', fig. 2). An ornamental boss of the Safavid period (fig. 6) or the underside of a Nasrid-period stirrup (figs 7, 8) display more centrally radial openwork designs.

Some carved vessels and urns feature an openwork layer set over an inner solid wall. The so-called Macy jug (dated 1215–16) is an example of medieval Iranian glazed

FIG. 5
Bronze openwork ornament,
Seljuq Iran, 12th century
The Metropolitan Museum of Art,
Rogers Fund, 1949, 49.60.2

FIG. 6
Bronze ornamental boss,
Safavid Iran, 16th century
The Metropolitan Museum of Art,
Gift of Arthur Jaffe, 1976, 1976.159.3

FIG. 7
Pair of enamelled stirrups, Nasrid
Spain, late 15th–early 16th century
The Metropolitan Museum of Art,
Gift of J. Pierpont Morgan, 1917,
17.190.642

FIG. 8
Underside of the stirrup showing
openwork pattern, Nasrid Spain,
late 15th–early 16th century
The Metropolitan Museum of Art,
Gift of J. Pierpont Morgan, 1917,
17.190.642

FIG. 5

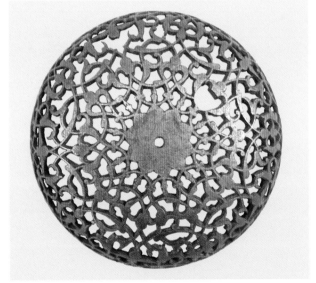

FIG. 6

FIG. 7

FIG. 8

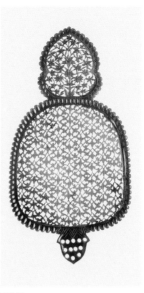

FIG. 9   FIG. 10   FIG. 11

FIG. 9
Double-walled ceramic ewer with openwork body, Kashan, Iran, dated AH 612 (1215–16)
The Metropolitan Museum of Art, Fletcher Fund, 1932, 32.52.1

FIG. 10
Double-walled bronze *lota* with openwork screen, northern India, 17th century
The Metropolitan Museum of Art, Purchase, Gift of George Blumenthal, by exchange, 1982, 1982.65

FIG. 11
Mirror frame, nephrite jade, Mughal style in Chinese central Asia, 18th century
The Metropolitan Museum of Art, Gift of Heber R. Bishop, 1902, 02.18.764

ceramic in this technique (fig. 9). Here, an organic pierced overlay of vines and stems contains figures of harpies, sphinxes and quadrupeds. A similar concept is seen in a bronze Mughal vase or *lota* of the seventeenth century, where an interior container is surrounded by an outer layer of openwork arabesques within an ogival trellis (fig. 10). Its *jali* body evokes the courtly buildings that it must have once occupied.

A nephrite jade mirror frame carved with fine arabesques and flowers (fig. 11) is an exquisite courtly object created in the *jali* mode. Attributed to Chinese central Asia, it demonstrates the wide reach of the Mughal aesthetic in the eighteenth century when jade carvers in that region referred to the 'Hindustan' style.[7] The visual interplay between such Mughal-style objects and various modes of ornament in architecture includes the art of stone inlay, relief carving, *jali* work and interior furnishings.[8] These forms often echo the variations of the same designs shown open, closed, rising or sunken into surfaces, creating a richness of related effects in a variety of mediums. ⊗

NOTES

1. *Howard Hodgkin: in conversation with David Sylvester*. Landseer / Arts Council of Great Britain, broadcast on London Weekend Television, 1982.

2. For recent scholarship on light in Islamic art, see, Bloom and Blair (eds), *Light of Heavens and Earth*, 2015.

3. Asher, *Architecture of Mughal India*, 108.

4. Stone, *Symbol of Divine Light*, 82, fig. 94.

5. Ibid., 84–102.

6. Koch, *Complete Taj Mahal*, 166.

7. Watt, "Bowl with Bud Handles," 368–69.

8. For a larger study of Mughal ornament, see, Michell, *Majesty of Mughal Decoration*, 2007.

Temple *Jali* Traditions

George Michell

From the earliest times in India, the saviours of Buddhism and Jainism and the gods and goddesses of Hinduism have been venerated in confined, dimly lit sanctuaries. These recall the environment of a natural cave, especially when artificially scooped out of a rugged rock face, but even when recreated out of stone blocks assembled in freestanding, constructed buildings. Worshippers gather in front of sanctuary doorways to chant prayers and make offerings, most often in halls that are spacious and well illuminated when compared with the sanctuaries. But the daylight flooding into temple interiors through doorways and windows is generally severe and requires filtering to be comfortably tolerated: hence the use of screens, popularly known as *jali*s. As an integral part of Indian sacred architecture, *jali*s imbue temple interiors with a soft and diffused light that encourages devotion, directing the attention of worshippers towards the emblem or image housed in the sanctuary.

Timber screens must have been in widespread use in the architecture of ancient India, but only the scantiest evidence of them survives due to the country's unforgiving climate, which erodes all organic materials. Even so, curved teak ribs more than 2,000 years old can still be seen in Buddhist prayer halls known as *chaitya*s, such as those at Kondane and Karla in the Western Ghats of India's Deccan region. These ribs once supported timber screens that modified the light entering through great arched openings. Stone relief imitations of these wooden screens, some with petalled lattice patterns, are set into the arched frames above doorways and windows of rock-cut Buddhist monuments, as in the rock-cut Buddhist *chaitya* hall at Bedsa (fig. 1) dating back to the second–first century BC.

Architects in India in later times seem never to have forgotten wooden screens such as these early examples from the Buddhist era. Stone *jali*s in the Hindu temples built from the fifth century AD onwards have multiple square openings defined by horizontal and vertical bars, occasionally reinforced by angled struts, which imitate bamboo or teak construction. Occasionally decorated with tiny lotus flowers and foliate bands, *jali*s of this type are present in the windows of the Parvati temple at Nachna in Madhya Pradesh, the Mundeshvari temple in Bihar and the Ladkhan

FIG. 2

temple at Aihole in Karnataka. In the latter monument, timber-like sandstone *jali*s are inserted into walls on three sides of a large hall to illuminate the town meetings that may have taken place here, while rites of worship were relegated to a small rooftop shrine above. The early eighth-century Galaganatha temple at Pattadakal, Karnataka, has a wall carving, depicting Shiva impaling a victim, set between *jali*s with diagonal perforations (fig. 2).

Over time, the square openings of *jali*s are rotated 45 degrees to create diagonal perforations, sometimes with indented profiles with stepped sides, as in the twelfth-century temples at Belur in Karnataka. Such modifications helped reduce the quantity of light admitted. A further innovation is the introduction of tiny lotuses, either as full blossoms with one or more rings of petals, or pointed, radial petals, or even as diamond-shaped flowers, all of which altered the light passing through the perforations. Swastika motifs imbued with auspicious powers make an early appearance in *jali* compositions, as in the eighth-century Durga temple in Aihole (fig. 3). Swastika *jali*s are even found in later times in Tamil Nadu, as in the windows of the sixteenth-century Subrahmanya shrine within the compound of the great Brihadishvara temple in Thanjavur. Intricate knotted designs must also have been considered as a suitable motif within a sacred monument, beginning with examples on the screens of the eighth-century Virupaksha temple at Pattadakal (fig. 4), even surviving into the fifteenth century, as in the *jali*s of the Krishna temple at Shamalaji in Gujarat.

Other geometric *jali* motifs include quarter-circles, triangles, tiny squares and cutout zigzag bands. These miscellaneous designs are sometimes combined to achieve a catalogue of perforated geometries, as in the relief panels representing *jali*s incorporated into the side walls of the grandly scaled, eleventh-century step-well at Patan in Gujarat. *Jali* motifs in fifteenth-century temples in the same region are sometimes combined to create screen walls encasing the outer halls of sacred monuments, as in the Neminatha temple (fig. 5) at the Jain holy mountain site of Girnar. An equally comprehensive catalogue of such motifs is displayed in the *jali*s of the similarly dated Parshvanatha temple in Lodruva in Rajasthan. As will be noticed in the next chapter, many of these designs also occur in the *jali*s of fifteenth- and sixteenth-century mosques and tombs. This sharing of geometric screen motifs between Hindu, Jain and Islamic monuments is a distinctive feature of architecture in Gujarat. Such commonalities are best explained by guilds of masons who sought employment under patrons of different backgrounds, often working at the same time on temples, mosques and tombs. *Jali*s with meticulously carved geometric patterns are also a characteristic of Hindu and Jain shrines in Rajasthan, as well as in residential mansions known as *haveli*s. The intricately worked *jali* balconies of

FIG. 2
Wall carving depicting Shiva impaling a victim set between *jali*s with diagonal perforations, Galaganatha temple, Pattadakal, Karnataka, early 8th century

FIG. 3
Jali with swastika design in the
colonnaded verandah, Durga
temple, Aihole, Karnataka, first half
of the 8th century

FIG. 4
*Jali*s with knotted designs,
Virupaksha temple, Pattadakal,
Karnataka, mid-8th century

FIG. 5

FIG. 5
Porch with *jali*s exhibiting a
catalogue of geometric and floral
design, Neminatha temple, Girnar,
Gujarat, 15th century

the *haveli*s in Jaisalmer serve to guarantee privacy to women of the household, permitting them to discreetly observe life on the streets below.

In addition to stylised lotuses and geometric patterns, temple *jali*s also draw on naturalistic vegetal designs, which in India are regarded as sources of magical protection. This is apparent in the windows of the Virupaksha temple at Pattadakal in Karnataka, many of which display leafy stems and foliate fronds interlocking in

imaginative, lifelike formations that express the exuberance of the natural world (fig. 6). Encircling vines inhabited by tiny dancers and musicians must also have been considered desirable, since they are often positioned beside sanctuary doorways, as in the eleventh-century Tripurakanteshvara temple at Balligave, Karnataka (fig. 7). Further south, in the Tamil country, *jali*s with swirling vines with miniature figures are also popular, judging from windows in the twelfth-century Airavateshvara temple in Dharasuram and seventeenth-century Kudal Alagar temple in Madurai.

FIG. 6
*Jali*s with fanciful foliate designs,
Virupaksha temple, Pattadakal,
Karnataka, mid-8th century

FACING PAGE
FIG. 7
Jali with dancers in scrolling
stalks, with monster masks above,
Tripurakanteshvara temple, Balligave,
Karnataka, 11th century

FIG. 8

Themes of nature also extend to peacocks with drooping foliate tails, wheels with multiple fish spokes, and even cobras with sinuous, interlocking bodies. The latter motif survives into more recent wooden *jali*s, such as the eighteenth-century example from coastal Karnataka (fig. 12), now in the Victoria and Albert Museum, London.

A striking innovation in *jali* design in Hindu religious architecture is the inclusion of figures cut out in almost three dimensions, as in the windows of the seventh-century Parashurameshvara temple at Bhubaneswar (fig. 8) in India's eastern state of Odisha. The hall of this small but exquisitely finished monument is lit by *jali*s carved with male dancers, their limbs energetically disposed as they vigorously pace out their steps to the accompaniment of flautists and drummers.

Several monuments in the Deccan lack niches to accommodate carvings of gods and goddesses; instead, such figures are incorporated into perforated windows. *Jali*s in the ninth-century Bhoganandishvara temple at Nandi show Shiva dancing on a prostrate demon, as well as the goddess Durga standing triumphantly on the head of the buffalo demon she has just decapitated. The Durga image is adorned with flowers since the *jali* is now treated as a votive icon. Other screens set into the walls of this monument show pot-bellied imps, known as *gana*s, who guard the treasures of the underworld. These creatures cavort in *jali*s with swirling vines framed by pilasters carrying ornamental aquatic monsters (fig. 9).

*Jali*s in the Chennakeshava temple in Belur, mentioned earlier, were added to partly enclose the interior by Ballala II, the Hoysala king and grandson of the building's royal founder. By this time, the temple's outer walls had altogether been covered with sculpted imagery (see p. 18), so the screens themselves are embellished with figural compositions arranged in panels or long bands running between indented square perforations. The *jali*s either side of the main entrance at Belur depict Ballala II seated with his queens, ministers, priestly advisors and retinue in a unique portrayal of formal audiences at the Hoysala court. Other screens at Belur have panels illustrating episodes drawn from popular legends, such as the gods and demons churning the cosmic ocean by pulling the great serpent Vasuki (fig. 10) or episodes from the mythology of Vishnu (fig. 11).

Mythological topics are also integrated into *jali*s that encase passageways surrounding Hindu shrines in the tropical western coast of India. The sixteenth–seventeenth-century Mahadeva temples in Kaviyur and Ettumanur in Kerala, for instance, preserve delicately worked timber *jali*s (fig. 13). These may have resembled wooden screens in Hindu monuments of earlier times elsewhere in India that are

FIG. 8
Jali with dancers and musicians, Parashurameshvara temple, Bhubaneswar, Odisha, mid-7th century

FIG. 9
Jali with dancers and musicians in a scrolling stalk emerging from watery foliation, Bhoganandishvara temple, Nandi, Karnataka, 9th century

FACING PAGE
FIG. 10
Jali screen with panel on top depicting churning of the cosmic ocean, Chennakeshava temple, Belur, Karnataka, 12th century

FOLLOWING PAGES
FIG. 11
Detail of a *jali* illustrating episodes from the mythology of Vishnu in his avatar as the giant Trivikrama pacing out the cosmic steps (middle band), Chennakeshava temple, Belur, Karnataka, 12th century

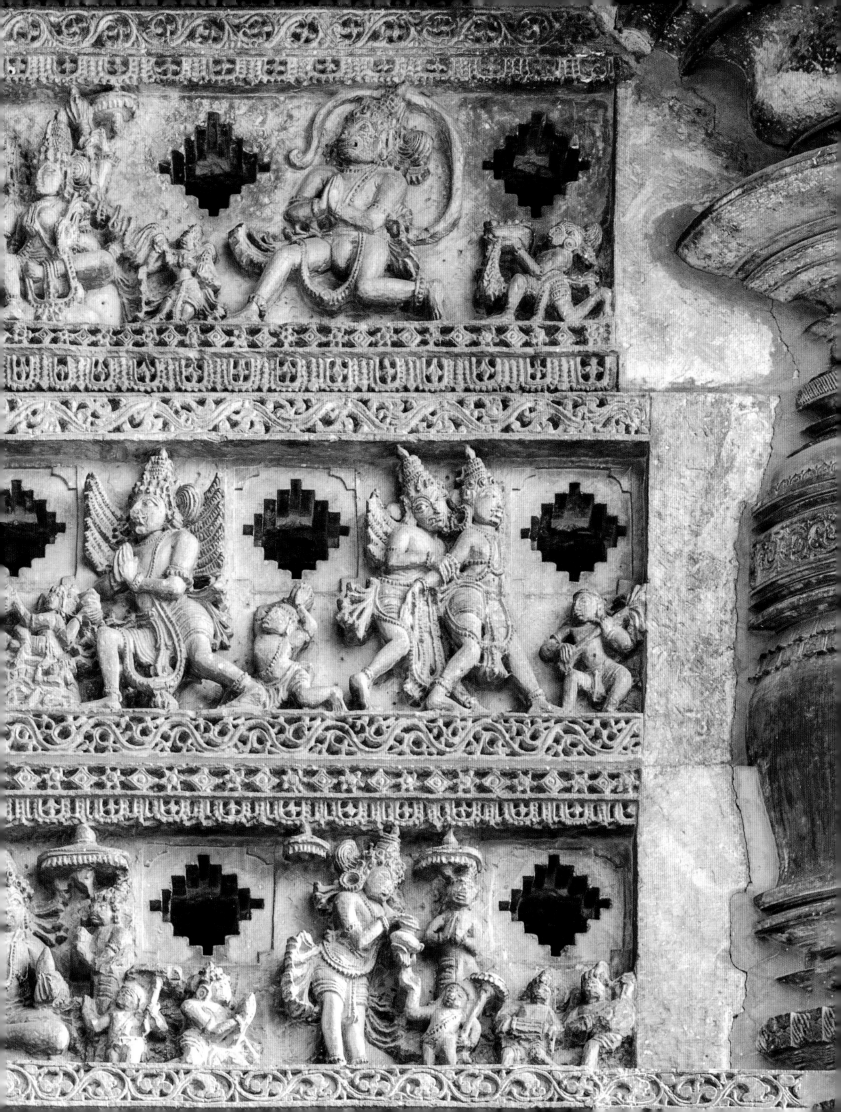

FIG. 13

no longer preserved. The Kerala *jali*s have multiple square openings relieved by tiny lotus blossoms, often interrupted by panels carved with Hindu divinities. At the doorways to the shrines, these divinities are replaced with fierce, armed guardians. This combination of geometric and floral *jali*s with figural compositions in the temples of Kerala creates richly textured wooden surfaces, which are vulnerable to weather. Here, as in other temples of the region, the *jali*s are sheltered from severe monsoon rains by overhanging, sloping tiled roofs. For this reason, they survive as unique testaments to India's mostly vanished, timber *jali* tradition. ⊗

Sacred Symbols
Jalis of the Gujarat Sultanate

"The naga-bandha *(snake-band), the* valli-bandha *(leaf-band), the* gavaksha *(cow's eye), the* kunjaraksha *(elephant's eye) and resembling the* svastika *(meander), the* sarvatobhadra, *and the* nandyavarta *shapes, and the* pushpa-bandha *(flower-band),… : these are the shapes of the windows of which the* naga *and the* valli *should be employed in temples."*[1]

Manasara Silpasastra, fourth century

❖ Temple *Jali*s and Their Auspicious Motifs

The elaborate adornment of Hindu and Jain temples involved many ornate features in stone carving. Stone was hewn and shaped into a wealth of relief designs, pendant forms, sculptural figures and miniaturized architectural motifs, all distinct elements in a temple's rich iconography. These included perforated screens and windows, which incorporate auspicious motifs and symbols relating to the wider iconographic programme of the building. Many of these forms evolved from earlier examples in timber (see previous essay by George Michell), which were later realized by artisans working in stone. Carving and drilling techniques allowed for heavy walls to be pierced in order to allow light into the interior space through lattices, often close to the circumambulatory zone surrounding the central chamber. Openwork lattices can also be found in square or rectangular windows around an entrance porch. The term *jali* (a diminutive of the Sanskrit term *jalaka*) finds its origins in these developments, as do the stone piercing and carving techniques and designs that were later adapted for use in Sultanate and Mughal architecture. Solanki–period temple *jali*s (eleventh to twelfth centuries) of Gujarat and Rajasthan had a particularly strong impact on the styles of the Sultanate period of the same region, bestowing their auspicious grid designs on later Islamic structures.[2]

The classification of temple *jali* designs and their symbolism has been expounded in modern studies.[3] A lexicon of Sanskrit terms for the individual designs implies that much of this nomenclature stayed unchanged over the centuries.[4] This would suggest that when later building styles such as mosques were outfitted with *jali*s, the same

FIG. 1

terminology may have continued in usage. The Sanskrit terms precisely identify a great range of *jali* designs in temples from very simple spaced vertical bars (*stambha jalaka*) to evermore elaborate forms. Auspicious Indian symbols include the meander shape (*swastika*) or meander with short curved arms (*nandyavarta*), goose (*hamsa*), conch shell (*shankha*), lion (*simha*) and medallion, sometimes composed of eight fish (*chakra-vyuha*).[5] Geometric forms (*bahurandhra*) are also known, among them variations of a simple pattern of drilled square holes, sometimes elaborated by a stepped treatment around the edge (*turyasra, chaturasraka, sarvatobhadra, sakarnaka, vardhaman*) or tipped to form a diamond-like pattern (*gonetra, gajendranayana*). Architectural features such as miniature columns—sometimes bearing a figural sculpture—or cross straps (*rjukriya* or *stambha*) also form a category of *jali*. A quite different type of *jali* takes a more fluid and naturalistic form, either vegetal or floral. An open flower-head in a hole (*pushpakhantha*) or a flowing or interlocked vine (*latayukta* or *valli jalaka*) are the most common. Other natural forms are derived from lotus leaf or petals (*padmapatra*) or leaf profiles (*patrajatika*). Among the figural styles are intertwined serpents (*nagabandha*) which usually interlock two symmetrically placed cobras around the edges or across the centre of an open square. Dancers or celestial beings (*gulika, sachitranga*) are also included in temple *jali*s, as are elephants, deer, auspicious vases, masks, and mythological creatures such as *yali*s. But of all the figural types, it is just a lone peacock or two that makes its way into Islamic buildings, for example at the shrine of Muhammad Ghaus in Gwalior.

From Temple to Mosque: Transformations in the *Jali*

With the development of Islamic styles of architecture in Gujarat from the fourteenth century, a new set of ideas transformed the relatively small-scale temple *jali* into a prominent feature in shrines and mosques. The symbolic importance of light in Islam, the need for discreet spaces in mosque enclosures (*maqsura*s) for women and elite visitors, as well as new aesthetic preferences for walls of lightness and pattern ushered in this change. The grid-like *jali* (so-called *sakhandaka*) found on the outer wall of a temple (fig. 1) was adapted and expanded in mosques and tombs, sometimes enclosing the entire building, and in particular the tomb chamber. This style of *jali* grid contains repeating squares, each one bearing an individual sacred symbol almost identical to those from Jain and Hindu temples. A few modest innovations were added to the received formula, most notably a series of openwork *mihrab*-arch shaped openings in the uppermost line.[6] The *jali* thus evolved from a minor feature to a key characteristic of the building. Gujarati Sultanate architecture is replete with extraordinary *jali* screens, serving as both decoration and function.

The architectural remains at Bharuch, Khambhat, and Dholka have some of the earliest Islamic buildings of Gujarat and important transitions in style and function

FIG. 1
Jali wall, Ajinatha Temple,
Taranga, Gujarat, 11th century

FOLLOWING PAGES
FIG. 2
Hilal Khan Qazi mosque, Dholka,
Gujarat, 1333

FIG. 3

FIG. 4

can be observed, including the transformation of the *jali* and the reuse of temple architectural elements. The mosque at Dholka, built in 1333 by Hilal Khan Qazi, a general of the Tughlaqs, features expansive *jali* screens in the upper level as well as in the *zenana* (women's quarter) area (fig. 2).[7] This early patron took steps to elevate the *jali* to a new status and function, developing an influential new formula. The temple whose elements are reused to build this mosque might have had some existing perforated screens that were added to. But even so we can see an adaptation of Islamic aesthetics in the introduction of arched openings in the top line of the upper screen (fig. 3). While most of the *jali*s are in the square-grid *sakhandaka* format, a new aesthetic effect is seen in the interplay of larger and smaller perforated surfaces around an arched window opening (fig. 4). There

FIG. 5

FIG. 6

is also an attempt to match openwork patterns to those on the *minbar*, which is ornamented on the sides with blind *jali* relief designs (fig. 5). On the roof we find an exterior view of rising *jali*s that would have brought in the light to the upper section of the interior space (fig. 6).

FIGs 3, 4, 5 & 6
Hilal Khan Qazi mosque, Dholka, Gujarat, 1333

A later monument at Dholka presents *jali*s fashioned in a distinctly Middle Eastern design. These perforated screens appear in the Alif Khan Bhukai mosque, a massive brick building dating from the period of Sultan Mahmud Begara (r. 1458–1511) noted for its foreign features.[8] The original structure consisted of two square solid minarets, one on each end of the facade. The mosque's interior consists of three square halls, each enclosed with a massive dome. The central *mihrab*, or prayer

FIG. 7
Jali screen, mosque of Alif Khan,
Dholka, Gujarat, c. 1450–60

FIG. 8
Wall panel with geometric interlace,
coloured stones and marble,
Mamluk Egypt or Syria, 15th century,
The Metropolitan Museum of Art,
Gift of the Hagop Kevorkian Fund,
1970, 1970.327.8

FIG. 9
Weathered screen, mosque of Alif
Khan, Dholka, Gujarat, c. 1450–60

FIG. 10
Carved plaster decoration with
interlace and floral medallions
above flowering pomegranate
tree, Mosque of Alif Khan, Dholka,
Gujarat, c. 1450–60

FIG. 8   FIG. 9   FIG. 10

niche, is flanked by two windows decorated with perforated stone tracery (fig. 7), while more such windows appear at a greater height along the wall. The perforated windows feature geometric star-based interlace designs of a kind that are almost ubiquitous in the western Islamic world, from Mamluk Egypt (fig. 8) to Nasrid Spain, appearing in window trellises, furniture, textile design and mosaic inlay but little known in India at this time. The stellate motifs are made up of overlapping rigid bands that extend from a central star and meet to form a broader medallion around it. The deep weathering of the trellises on the Alif Khan mosque (fig. 9) suggests that they are original and are not replacements added at a later time. The exotic designs of the window traceries also echo in the cut and carved stucco ornament of the building. Areas of the exterior walls are ornamented with deeply carved designs, mainly roundels, scrolling and foliate forms, which have a distinct character and composition displaying Middle Eastern influence. Among them are spiral lappets, wispy lotus heads, exuberant bushes and a flowering pomegranate tree (fig. 10).

Located on the Sabarmati river, the city of Ahmedabad was founded in 1411 by Sultan Ahmad Shah. This new capital of Gujarat developed rapidly with the palace as the nucleus, encircled by commercial districts. The vigorous building activity of his successors, including the dynamic Mahmud Begara, ushered in a new phase of architecture with striking aesthetic effects that united Islamicate and Indic forms. Among them was an arched window containing motifs enclosed in squares. This adaptation of a square grid set under a curving arch presented an elegant framework but also certain design challenges, which were admirably met in subtle variations of design and proportion. *Jali* windows from the Rani no Hajiro complex, comprising eight marble tombs of queens of Ahmad Shah I and other Sultanate rulers in

FIG. 12

FIG. 13

FIG. 14

FIGs 11, 12, 13 & 14
Jali windows and rails, Rani no Hajiro complex, Ahmedabad, c. 1450

Ahmedabad, show a drama of geometry and silhouette. Arched windows enclose patterns of triangular repeats (fig. 11), meander and geometric motifs (fig. 12), and bold designs of medallions (fig. 13). These also appear on carved railings (fig. 14).

The Rani Sipri (more accurately Rani Sabrai) Roza, a mosque and tomb complex, named after the queen of Sultan Mahmud Begara, is located just inside the Astodia Gate of the old walled city of Ahmedabad. An inscription dates the structure to the year 1514. The mosque is a rectangular building, closed on three sides and open on the east side where it adjoins a paved square. The open east facade is framed by two ornately carved minarets that take the form of engaged pillars, tapering as they rise to a height well above the roof. The interior of the mosque has three *mihrab*s along the back wall, and two ornately screened windows allow light to pass through this wall into the building. The tomb, situated directly opposite the mosque, is a square pavilion with a central domed chamber surrounded by an ambulatory. The outer walls of the ambulatory are screened with *jali* work (fig. 15), enclosing the tomb chamber in a web of light and pattern. The femininity of this monument is conveyed by the veil-like *jali* screens that play a prominent role in rendering its delicate character. Such architectural features begin to make their way into paintings. An early sixteenth-century folio from a dispersed illustrated manuscript of the *Chandayana* of Mulla Da'ud depicts a palace interior with women. The lower register of the composition contains a pointed arch with a grid of open squares (fig. 16) to indicate a *jali* screen

FIG. 15
Rani Sipri tomb complex, Ahmedabad, Gujarat, 1514

FIG. 16
A *jali* doorway leading into women's quarters, detail of a folio from a dispersed manuscript of the *Chandayana*, early 16th century, The Metropolitan Museum of Art Purchase, Cynthia Hazen Polsky Gift, 1990, 1990.82

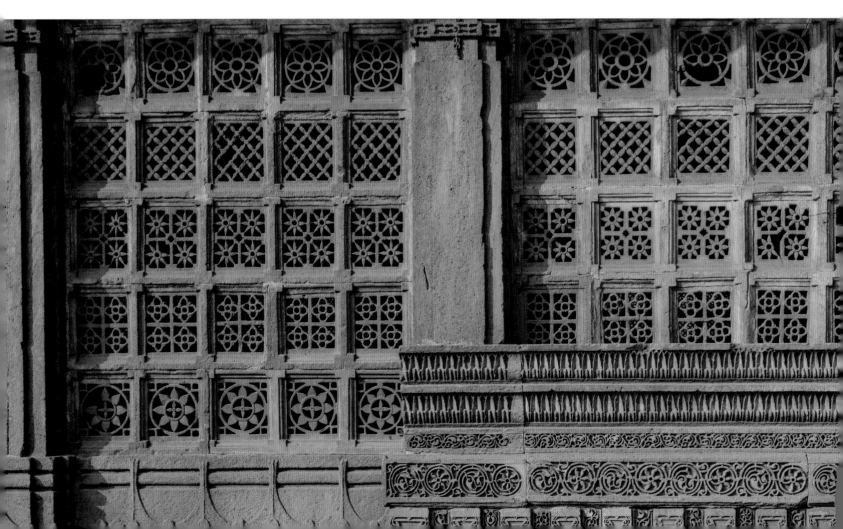

or doorway shielding the women's quarters. This simple metallic grid style had an elevated status in shrines and mosques, such as a window grille dated 1488 from the mausoleum founded by Azmadur Mazid al-Ashrafi in Aleppo (fig. 17).

The transformative effect of *jali*s encircling a tomb chamber can be seen in the Sarkhej Roza near Ahmedabad, the mid-fifteenth century tomb complex of the Sufi saint Shaikh Ahmad Khattu, known as Ganj Bakhsh (fig. 18). Construction on the complex took place during the reigns of Muhammad Shah II (r. 1442–1451) and Mahmud Shah I (r. 1458–1511). The Persian brothers 'Azam and Mu'azzam Khan are credited as the architects of the Sarkhej Roza. The tomb and mosque complex on the northeastern side of the tank is the oldest part of the assemblage. The tomb is a domed cubical chamber that opens onto a paved terrace surrounding the structure. On the south terrace, a hypostyle pavilion links the terrace immediately around the tomb and a lower paved area, accessed by broad stairs on three sides of the pavilion. The Sarkhej Roza complex has a wealth of pierced *jali*s. The upper and lower sections of the surrounding walls of the prayer hall are pierced and patterned, endowing the outer appearance of the building with lightness and creating dramatic contrasts of light and shadow within. *Mihrab* niches in the interior are filled with spectacularly carved floral ornament and bathed all around in the pierced light of *jali*s and reflections on the floor (fig. 19). Whether seen in silhouette (fig. 20) or viewed from the exterior, the drama and variety of repeating motifs and their visual effects are to be admired.

FIG. 17
Wrought-iron window grille, Aleppo, Syria, 893 AH / 1488
Al Sabah Collection, Kuwait, LNS 128M

FIG. 16

FIG. 17

FIG. 18

FIG. 19

FIG. 20

FIG. 18
Sarkhej Roza mosque, Ahmedabad,
Gujarat, 1451

FIG. 19
Interior of Sarkhej Roza mosque

FIG. 20
Jali screen, Sarkhej Roza mosque

FIG. 21
Jali details from the Sarkhej Roza
mosque and Shah-i 'Alam Roza
mosque and tomb complex,
Ahmedabad, Gujarat

Shah-i 'Alam Roza is a large mosque and tomb complex located southeast of the old city centre of Ahmedabad. It commemorates the burial place of the Sufi saint Muhammad Shah-i 'Alam (d. 1475), son of Abd-allah Qutb-i 'Alam Bukhari. The complex contains Shah-i 'Alam's tomb, another large tomb, a mosque, a cistern, an ablutions tank, and an assembly hall or guest house (*diwan-khana*). The buildings in Shah-i 'Alam Roza are dated to various times, spanning from as early as the period after his death during the reign of Mahmud Shah I (d. 1511), and up until the early seventeenth century. The main tomb itself sits on a raised platform, the central chamber of which is surrounded by a double ambulatory formed by an inner and outer colonnade. The spaces between the outer pillars are bridged by arches filled with carved marble screens creating outer walls. Shah-i 'Alam's grave is surrounded by *jali*s that filter the light onto the cenotaph (fig. 22). The delicate and exquisite quality of the carving and the inventive arrangement of designs makes this tomb one of the finest examples of funerary design.

The architectural remains at Champaner, about 150 km from Ahmedabad, include a number of important Sultanate buildings. Among them lies the Jami Masjid, built in 1523, as well as several other edifices (see p. 38). This rectangular mosque with an open courtyard has a plan that is similar to the Jami Masjid in Ahmedabad, built 75 years earlier. The prayer hall of the mosque is covered by eleven domes with the central part of the roof raised on a further two storeys of pillared arcades. The main entrance to the courtyard of the mosque on the east side is in the form of a large domed portico raised on a podium with steps on the north and south sides. Each side once had perforated stone windows, and on the east side there was a projecting balcony, of which only the floor has survived. The dome has collapsed and only two of the four *chhatri*s can be seen, but enough of the *jali*s survive to give a sense of the lightness and airiness of the entrance way into the mosque (fig. 23). The charm and elegance of this portico, whose ornament sparkles in the sunshine, are testament to the aesthetic power of the *jali*, which dapples this space with light. Ornately carved windows are pleasingly composed, offering a view of greenery framed in carved ornament, and surmounted with pierced arches that provide glimpses of the sky above.

The imposing Sehar ki Masjid, possibly built as a private royal mosque at Champaner in the late fifteenth century, is a long structure with five *mihrab*s, each surmounted by a dome. It also contains one powerful *jali* on one of the *jharokha*s (fig. 24) that flank the entrance. Bearing a strongly geometric stepped square design that resembles a Patan ikat-woven textile, the deeply cut stone is a marvel of technique and drama (fig. 25).

PREVIOUS PAGES
FIG. 22
Interior of Tomb of Shah-i 'Alam,
Ahmedabad, Gujarat, 1575

FIG. 23
Portico, Jami Masjid, Champaner,
Gujarat, 1523

FIG. 24 & FIG. 25 (FOLLOWING PAGES)
Jali window, Sehar ki Masjid,
Champaner, Gujarat,
late 15th century

PREVIOUS PAGES
FIG. 26
Tree of Life *jali*, Sidi Sayyid Mosque,
Ahmedabad, Gujarat, 1572–73

FIG. 27
Relief carving at Rani Sipri
tomb complex, Ahmedabad,
Gujarat, 1514

FIG. 27

FIG. 28

However, without doubt the masterpiece of all Gujarati *jali*s are of a type that stand apart for their lyricism and virtuosity—the Tree of Life carved screens of the Sidi Sayyid Mosque in Ahmedabad. The building was previously attributed to the patronage of a slave of Ahmad Shah I (r. 1411–1442) but is now attributed to an Abyssinian nobleman of the time of Sultan Muzaffar III (r. 1561–1572). Within the mosque enclosure, the *qibla* wall and side walls contain a series of almost semi-circular arches. The upper sections of the arches are fitted with exquisitely carved *jali*s, particularly the two that flank the central *mihrab*. This pair of *jali*s is each carved with the central motif of a tree, different from each other but unified in overall style. One contains a magnificent blossoming tree whose outwardly curving branches form gracious and pleasingly asymmetrical floral arabesques, standing before an almost hidden straight palm tree (fig. 26). The other *jali* contains a taller and slimmer central tree with sinuously interlocked branches, flanked by smaller waving date palms with chevron trunks and flowering trees, each with distinct types of blossoms (see pp. 6–7). Seven other perforated screens on the back and side walls of the building are regally carved in the square-grid style.

The 'Tree of Life' imagery reflects the importance of the tree motif as an ancient symbol of protection, fertility and divinity in Indian art and architecture. Images of the wish-fulfilling tree (*kalpavriksha*) and auspicious vines (*vallijatika*) and leaves (*patrajatika*) appear widely in architectural ornament (fig. 27).[9] Flowering trees in mosque and tomb decoration evoke the Tree of Immortality (*shajarat al-khuld*) or the Blessed Tree in Paradise (*tuba*) mentioned in the Qur'an, or other metaphorical and actual trees described in Islamic literary and poetic tradition. The Sidi Sayyid *jali*s therefore blend the ideals of Indian and Islamic beneficence through their multi-layered and richly inflected arboreal imagery and powerful aesthetic language. Such fecund motifs exist all over Gujarati architecture, including in the sensitively carved trees adorning the cenotaph of Umar bin Ahmad al Kazeruni in Khambhat (1333) (fig. 28). Yet the perceptible leap into a softer naturalism and decorative grace also reflects the influence of new aesthetics developing at the distant Mughal court in Delhi on the eve of Gujarat's annexation in 1573.

FIG. 28
Trees carved in relief on the cenotaph of Umar bin Ahmad al Kazeruni, Khambhat, Gujarat, 1333

❖ The Gujarat *Jali* Style in Evolution and Circulation

Gujarati *jali*s evolved new styles through the seventeenth to nineteenth centuries. Floral carving came to the fore, partly under Mughal influence, as did a greater degree of pure geometric design, displacing the earlier sacred motifs. Opulent arabesques and floral decorations over carved and pierced surfaces characterize the tombs of the Babi rulers of Junagadh (fig. 29). Wooden *jali* work became a hallmark of Gujarati *haveli*s and domestic interiors and *jali* carving styles were applied to

FIG. 29

FIG. 29
Tombs of the Babi rulers, Junagadh, Gujarat, 18th and 19th centuries

FIG. 30
Wooden casket with carved floral and geometric closed *jali* design, Ahmedabad, probably 17th century
Private collection, Ahmedabad

FIG. 31
Aina Mahal, Bhuj, Gujarat, 18th century

FIG. 30

FIG. 31

FIG. 32

furniture and objects as well. A richly carved wooden cabinet in a private collection in Ahmedabad features deep squares, some enclosing foliate and organic forms and others with regular geometric-based patterns (fig. 30). The Aina Mahal in Bhuj, built in the eighteenth century by Rao Lakhpatji, features floral carved *jali*s in stucco as well as wooden geometric trellises in the *jharokha* balconies (fig. 31).

The impact of Gujarati styles of art and architecture has been felt all around the Indian Ocean rim for centuries. The manufacture and export of carved marble tombstones from Khambhat to east Africa and southeast Asia in the late medieval period reveals a pattern of exchange that likely applied to other goods as well.[10] Gujarati textiles dating to as early as the fourteenth century have been located in collections in Fustat, Egypt, as well as Indonesia.[11] Among them is a type of painted and printed textile (fig. 32) featuring a characteristically shaped three-petalled floral blossom on a curving stem (the so-called Big Leaf style). This distinctive motif makes a rare appearance in a *jali* window square (fig. 33) in the mosque of Ahmad Shah at Ahmedabad (1414), demonstrating the fluid exchange of styles and symbols across media and region. The movement of Gujarati craftsmen across the Indian Ocean continued well into the nineteenth century, partly facilitated by

FIG. 32
Big Leaf-style textile from Gujarat for the Indonesian market, late 14th, early 15th century
The Metropolitan Museum of Art Purchase, Friends of Asian Art Gifts, 2005, 2005.407

FIG. 33
Jali window with textile-like motifs, mosque of Ahmad Shah, Ahmedabad, Gujarat, c. 1414

FIG. 34
Doorway with floral carved Gujarati-style lunette in Stone Town, Zanzibar, Tanzania

FIG. 33

FIG. 34

the administration of the British Raj. Therefore, it is not surprising to find styles of Gujarati carving in the nineteenth-century architecture, particularly doors and arches of the houses, in Stone Town in Zanzibar. Among the many designs seen are doors surmounted with an arch containing a deeply wrought perforated floral *jali* design (fig. 34), recalling those of the wooden *haveli*s and doorways of Ahmedabad, Khambhat and other cities of Gujarat.[12]

Tribal traditions of India offer preservation of historical memory and breathe a vibrant reinterpretation and new life into old forms of *jali*. These traditions are all the more commendable in light of the challenges of modernity for the tribal craftsman and artist. A remarkable tribal *jali* from Chhattisgarh made of mud and plaster (fig. 35) by a local female artist bears a close resemblance to the screens of the Gujarat Sultanate. A central panel with an arch is flanked by two others, all containing a grid of squares with motifs. Some of the motifs, such as the floral medallions, are recognizably descended from early *jalis*, while others, such as the tree or spool forms, come from the more informal decorative styles of rural India.

The influence of the Gujarat Sultanate *jali* lasted into the twentieth century, becoming a feature of the 'Indo-Saracenic' style of architecture. The Gateway of India monument in Bombay (now Mumbai), built to commemorate the landing of King George V and Queen Mary in 1911, features perforated screens brought from Gwalior (fig. 36). Their distinctive grid style with open ornament in each square recalls the hallmark style of Gujarati *jali*s. ⊗

PREVIOUS PAGES
FIG. 35
Contemporary *jali* screen by tribal artist Babi Sonwani Lakhanpur village, Chhattisgarh, 2019

FIG. 36
Gateway of India, Mumbai, 1915

NOTES

1. Acharya, *Architecture of Manasara*, 36–337.

2. Further afield, structures in southeast Asia, such as the fourteenth-century Panataran temples of eastern Java, were also carved with similar features.

3. Dhaky, *Indian Temple Traceries*, 2005; R Nath, *Architecture of Fatehpur Sikri*, 1988.

4. Tillotson, "Review of *Indian Temple Traceries* by Dhaky," 369–371, makes note of the geographic and temporal discrepancy between the cited literature and the extant architecture.

5. The swastika motif also appears in the art of the Middle East as a meander form evolving from classical ornament. The Metropolitan Museum of Art collections contain several examples, such as a Coptic Egyptian wall panel (07.228.38) and a Persian bowl with central rounded meander (1980.540).

6. Lambourn, "A self-conscious art?" 121–56, interprets this feature as 'micro-architecture'.

7. Burgess, *Muhammadan Architecture in Gujarat*, 30–33, provides description, plan and images of the mosque.

8. Burton-Page, "Sultanate Architecture," 15, suggests it is the work of foreign builders.

9. Dhaky, *Indian Temple Traceries*, figs 132–140.

10. Lambourn, "Carving and Communities," 99–133.

11. Barnes, *Indian Block-Printed Textiles in Egypt*, 1997.

12. For more on east African architecture and exchange see, Meier, *Swahili Port Cities*, 2016.

Celestial Geometry
Jalis of the Northern and Central Sultanates

"No ! I swear by the stars that recede, shifting and setting! By the night when it departs! By the morning when it breathes!"

Qur'an, 81:15-18

❖ Stars, Sun and Light in Islamic Architecture

Islamic architecture is replete with allusion to heavenly order and divinely inspired design. From this heritage come the stellate interior shape and decoration of domes and *muqarna*s (stalactite squinches) along with their association with the vault of heaven.[1] Architectural decoration incorporates astral features and interlace patterns that evoke the emanation of light in a starry sky. Solar medallions spread their radiance from the interior ornament of domes to the *shamsa*s (sunbursts) of manuscript illumination, carpet design and wood carving. While the meaning and styles of such features evolved in complex ways in relation to region, material, theological belief and the evolution of geometric patterns, nevertheless the motif of a star interwoven with polygonal forms became prominent over time. Varieties of stellar motifs appear in railings, grilles and window traceries in almost all parts of the Islamic world.[2]

The sophisticated treatment of light is also a hallmark of Islamic architectural spaces.[3] Light is shaped, diffused, reflected and filtered in buildings with visual, practical and symbolic intent.[4] Lustrous materials and shimmering pools of water act as mirrors from which images are reflected.[5] The changing interplay of light and shadow on relief-carved surfaces constantly transforms an edifice throughout the day and through the seasons. Light is also directed through perforated screens into sharp beams and dappled patterns while windows filled with geometric tracery provide starry silhouettes. This metaphoric relationship between symbols of light and light itself is a powerful dimension of Islamic art. Mamluk glass lamps, for example, frequently bear the Light Verse (*surat an-nur*); the clear letters written against a painted ground allow their message to be illuminated from within. Similarly, the outlines of stars in the domes of a bathhouse (*hammam*) or within interlace windows glow with the very light they seek to shape.

FACING PAGE
Ala'i Darwaza,
Qutb Minar complex,
Delhi, 1312

FIG. 1

FIG. 2

FIGs 1 & 2
Two marble window screens
from the Caliphate period,
Spain, 980–90
Museo Arquelogico Provincial
de Cordoba, 3.488

Lattice or tracery windows and larger ornamental or functional screens can be found in many examples of early and medieval Islamic architecture.[6] A comprehensive survey of these features within a wider view of the visual and theoretical study of Islamic ornament yet remains to be done.[7] The transmigration of motifs across inlay woodwork, carpet and textile designs and interior and exterior carved and painted decoration creates a world of inter-related ornament of which windows and screens are an integral part, while the dialogue between a veil of decoration and the structural skeleton of buildings fostered dynamic geometric schemes.[8] Yet designs, patterns and ideas also evolved in independent ways, oscillating between regional and imported tradition, reflecting the influence of courtly aesthetics and poetics.[9] The Topkapi Scroll, a late-Timurid era set of architectural drawings, has opened perspectives on the subject from the point of view of the designers and artisans of these accomplished idioms.[10] It also offers insight into the workings of angular interlace (*girih*)—a pattern of knots or nodal points that often coincided with the centre of stars or polygons—and its three-dimensional counterpart (*muqarnas*) in the pre-Mongol and post-Mongol Middle East. But it was a simple star-and-hexagon geometric pattern (*girih-sazi*) that first emerged in Delhi Sultanate *jali*s.[11]

Two large interlace marble window screens attributed to tenth-century Cordoba, possibly from a palace, provide evidence of an early elite style developed in Caliphate Spain. One is a hexagon-based design, the other is a more complicated set of interlocking geometrical forms with prominent stars (figs 1, 2). Together they have been interpreted as representing the coexistence of a classical and anti-classical vision—the first aspires for intellectual clarity and order, and the second aims to excite and puzzle with its underlying complexity.[12] Umayyad buildings in the eastern Mediterranean also incorporate interlace windows.[13] The Great Mosque of Damascus of the early eighth century features a row of small arched marble windows with geometric grilles set below the mosaics in the portico, of which four original examples survive. Their designs include one type based on circles set on a diagonal grid and another with intersecting trellises and geometric openings, outlined in grooved and overlapping ropey lines. Another Umayyad building, Qasr al-Hayr al-Gharbi, a rural palatine residence and agricultural compound located in the Syrian desert, was also decorated with pierced screens and panels. A series of largely reconstructed lunettes from the site, now in the National Museum, Damascus, feature a variety of openwork vegetal forms and geometric star-and-knot piercings.[14] Although we need not interpret these early architectural developments as the defining foundations for distant developments in the future, they nevertheless provide evidence of interlace windows and lunettes as a feature of sacred and secular early Islamic spaces.

Windows could be relatively small in relation to the wall in which they were set, remaining enclosed within arches and columns such as in a pre-Islamic pierced stucco window screen excavated at Qasr-i-Abu Nasr (fig. 3). This window from an octagonal-domed building features crenellations, engaged columns and rounded holes. In the centuries of building that followed, window grilles with geometric interlace became an established feature of architecture in the central Islamic lands, developing diverse visual effects in a variety of styles and materials. Patterns evolved in concert with the rest of the decorative programme of a given building and, generally speaking, over time the circles that were prominent early on gave way to repeating stars and radiating medallions. This perhaps reflected the advancing position of the Islamic mathematical sciences in the medieval age as the rounded and leafy designs of late antiquity became increasingly remote over time. Gradually, buildings around the Mediterranean and the Holy Land came to favour styles of window grilles with polygonal strap-work enclosing stars with multiple points to form rounded medallions that dominate the design, sometimes with interwoven

FIG. 3
Window screen, possibly Sasanian, Qasr-i Abu Nasr, Iran, c. 6th–7th century, stucco, The Metropolitan Museum of Art, Rogers Fund, 1933
33.175.37

FIG. 4
Stucco window detail, *bimaristan* of Nur al-Din in Damascus, Syria, 1154

FIG. 5
Rose window (detail) at the cathedral of Troia in Apulia, Italy, early 12th century

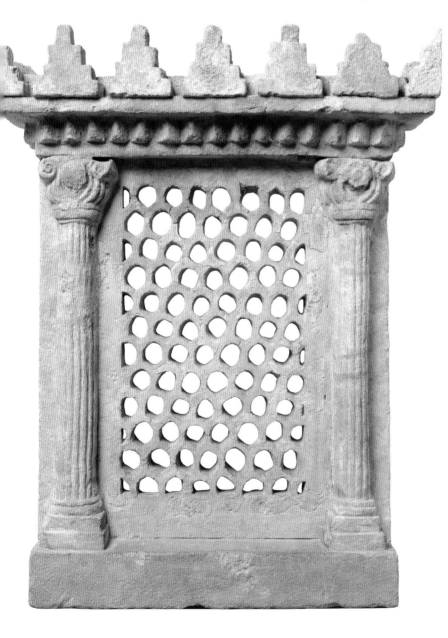

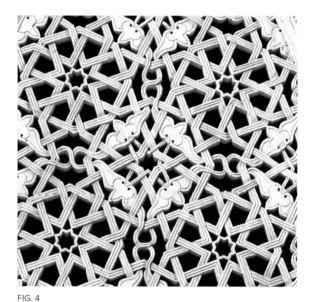

FIG. 4

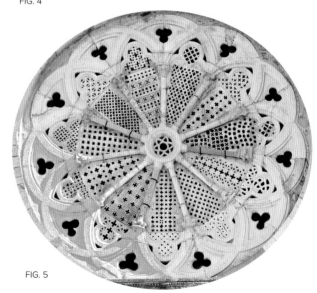

FIG. 5

FIG. 6

FIG. 6
Detail of *A Lady Receiving Visitors
(The Reception)*, by John Frederick
Lewis, oil on panel, 1873
Yale Center for British Art,
New Haven

stylized palmettes. A stucco window screen (fig. 4) in the hospital (*bimaristan*) built by the Zengid sultan Nur al-Din in Damascus in 1154 contains a network of triple fillets in octagonal geometry, bordered by acanthus leaves and large circles of simple, very flat palmettes entwined through the geometric pattern. These developments must have played a role in the evolution of rose windows in medieval cathedrals, as seen in the '*mudejar*' style of Santa Maria at Guadeloupe or the perforated rose window in the cathedral of Troia in Apulia, Italy[15] (fig. 5), which has been noted for its 'eastern style' fretwork.

Elaborate wooden grids (*mashribiyya*) that ornamented and protected residences became a distinctive feature of urban architecture, seen in the cities of Cairo and

FIG. 7

Damascus, among others. Their decorative effects caught the interest of several nineteenth-century artists whose naturalistic painting techniques were able to convey the atmosphere created by dappled light and shadows. *Mashribiyya* screens became a notable feature in the art of the English orientalist painter John Frederick Lewis (1804–76), one-time resident of Cairo. *The Reception*, made in 1873, captures the play of light through wooden screens and coloured glass windows into the chambers of an elite lady (fig. 6).[16] In a painting by the Turkish orientalist Osman Hamdi Bey (1842–1910), we see a sensitivity to the idea of filtered light that is in keeping with an Islamic point of view. *Young Woman Reading* depicts a woman reading in front of a window filled with interlace stars, the composition arranged so that the filtered light falls directly on the pages of her book of verses or prayers (fig. 7).[17]

Jalis of the Delhi Sultanate

The sultanate courts of northern India, particularly the Delhi Sultanate (1206–1555), ushered in new aesthetic tastes and forms of building and decoration from the Islamic west, which initially disrupted and eventually harmonized with local traditions. The Qutb Minar complex developed in Delhi at the turn of the thirteenth century by Qutb al-din Aibak (r. 1206–1210) and completed by his successors inaugurates many spectacular and influential features. These include the tall minaret itself with its styles of calligraphic and relief ornament, and the adjoining mosque earlier begun with the spolia of the existing temples on the site. Subsequent additions to the site

FIG. 7
Young Woman Reading,
by Osman Hamdi Bey, 1880
©Islamic Arts Museum Malaysia

FOLLOWING PAGES
FIG. 8
Ala'i Darwaza, Qutb Minar complex,
Delhi, 1312

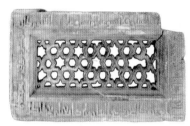

FIG. 9

FIG. 9
Marble screen with star-and-hexagon pattern, excavated at Ghazni, Afghanistan, first half of the 11th century
The Italian Archaeological Mission in Afghanistan

include the Ala'i Darwaza, the only surviving structure of four such gateways added by Ala al-Din Khalji (r. 1296–1316). Located on the southeastern edge of the complex, its elaborate treatment suggests that it may have been used as a gate to the city itself through the extension of the Qutb Mosque. Among the distinguished features of the Ala'i Darwaza are powerful *jali*s set within the monument's formidably thick walls (fig. 8 and see, p. 74).

The *jali* screens of the Ala'i Darwaza appear entirely different in spirit and style from the earlier temple *jali* styles that had developed in western India. These screens incorporate a classic 'Islamicate' geometric design—an alternating six-pointed star-and-hexagon pattern—as the main repeating motif. They are also long and slender in shape and placed within arched openings. Their patterns echo the relief carvings on the adjoining walls in a contrasting yet continuing effect that is a hallmark of many Islamic spaces. The bands that form the *jali* are stepped and grooved so that they have depth and dimension, an essential feature of the best screens and a mark of the carver's skills. Where can we find the most direct inspiration for these features? Like the Qutb Minar, which resembles the minarets of Jam at Ghor, the *jali*s of the Ala'i Darwaza demonstrate a style that possibly was adapted through exchanges with Ghurid and Ghaznavid Afghanistan.

Excavations at Ghazni at the site of the palace of Mas'ud III have yielded a group of pierced marble screens, some bordered with Arabic inscriptions in Kufic relief. One similar screen found re-employed at the Masjid Abu'l Fath, Arg (in Kabul) features the same star-and-hexagon pattern with grooved details (fig. 9) as those in the Ala'i Darwaza *jali*s. The palace, built in 1112 by the Ghaznavid sultan Mas'ud III (r. 1099–1114), son of Mahmud of Ghazna (or Ghazni), was probably burnt down during the Ghurid conquest of Ghazni in 1151; the city and the palace were demolished in 1221 by the Mongolian army of Genghis Khan. The palace ruins have been excavated by Italian archaeologists from Istituto Italiano per il Medio ed Estremo Oriente (IsMEO) who propose a reconstruction of the original scheme and suggest a placement for the inscribed screens on a prayer pulpit (*minbar*) in the mosque area.[18] This *minbar* would have likely had a flat top and lobed arches, possibly supported on two sides by pierced screens. Cursive inscriptions on the borders around the *jali*s provide information about the architect of the site. In the hands of Indian carvers, however, the carved and pierced geometry has been executed with greater finesse than the earlier versions at Ghazni.

Also at the Qutb complex in Delhi, the decorative and calligraphic features of the mausoleum of Iltutmish expand the range of the ornamental styles of Delhi Sultanate architecture. Located in the northwest corner of the complex next to the

FIG. 10

Sultan's own extensions to the Qutb Mosque, the simple cuboid structure built in 1235 is open on three sides. It has lost its dome and thus light streams in from above, illuminating the carvings on the interior walls. Constructed mainly of sandstone, the entrance and parts of the exterior are laid with quartzite; however, the real decorative richness of the tomb is found within. Elaborate epigraphy, arabesques, geometrical designs and Hindu motifs such as lotus flowers and bells on chains are found in the sandstone carvings. The *qibla* wall of the square sandstone tomb contains three *mihrab*s, the tall, central one made out of marble. Its lower interior section is pierced with quatrefoil lozenges set around a large lotus medallion at the centre (fig. 10). This square-based blind *jali* of Seljuqate inspiration echoes the rhythms of the calligraphic mirrored script in the arch above and the knotted designs found in the decorative carving all around.[19] The idea of a pierced marble panel within a *mihrab* interior, although rare, is also seen in Kairouan. Its ninth-century Great Mosque contains a *mihrab* constructed with several pierced marble panels, mainly foliate designs.[20]

FIG. 10
Detail of *mihrab* (prayer niche),
Tomb of Iltutmish, Qutb Minar
complex, Delhi, 1235

FIG. 12

Further away in the Qutb complex beside the eastern gateway of the Ala'i Darwaza is the light-filled tomb of Imam Zamin, built almost two hundred years later. According to the carved inscriptional panel above the entrance, the saint Imam Zamin came to India from Turkestan during the reign of Sikandar Lodi (r. 1489–1517), building this mausoleum in his lifetime. The tomb shares several architectural and stylistic features with the royal tombs of the Lodi dynasty, but little evidence of *jali*s survives at those other sites. Here, low walls are almost all in the form of perforated screens made up of flattened long straight lines which intersect to form small stars (fig. 11).

Powerfully austere *jali*s in a deep square grid are found in the Khirki Masjid (1351), or Mosque of Windows, thus named for the forty windows that decorate the upper floors (fig. 12). Located in the settlement of Jahanpanah, Delhi, the mosque is attributed to the commission of the dynamic builder Khan-i Jahan Junan Shah, vizier to the Tughluq sultan Firoz Shah (r. 1351–1388). The likely reason for its many windows is that the building has the distinction of being the first almost entirely covered mosque of north India, therefore requiring illumination through window openings. But it also has the character of a strong fortification, the formidably thick *jali*s adding to that impression. Local people of the region refer to it as a *qila* or fortress rather than a mosque.[21]

PREVIOUS PAGES

FIG. 11
Tomb of Imam Zamin, Qutb Minar complex, Delhi, 1538

FIG. 12
Khirki Masjid, Delhi, 1351

FIG. 13

❖ Beyond Delhi

*Jali*s of the sultanates of Jaunpur, Mandu, Sindh, Kashmir and elsewhere often share the cosmopolitan mode of Delhi with vernacular styles, representing varied encounters in ornamentation between Persianate and local Indian traditions. Across this wide landscape a number of interesting *jali*s deserve mention. The architecture commissioned by Baha al-din Tughrul, who was in power in the region of Bayana, Rajasthan, from 1195–1210, provides examples of some early modes of decoration. The lacy scrolling border of the *mihrab* arch of the late-twelfth century Chaurasi Khambha (84 pillars) mosque at Kaman in Rajasthan (fig. 13) is among them.[22] This mosque is built from spolia from earlier Hindu temples, as demonstrated in the profusion of reused pillars around the courtyard. However, the *mihrab* arch would have been carved as a new element, introducing a pointed arch shape and featuring bands of Arabic calligraphy. The arch itself is outlined with bands of scrolling vegetal ornament, the outermost of which is a delicate pierced edging of trefoil buds on a vine. While this feature cannot be considered to be a *jali* as such, it nevertheless provides an interesting and relevant insight into the aesthetic tastes that were developing in new features of architecture of the region. The nearby mosque of Ukha Mandir also has a similar *mihrab*, and its interior also preserves larger *jali* screens which surround the prayer space for women as well as a star-and-hexagon screen placed above the arch on the eastern facade.[23]

FIG. 13
Pierced scroll edge of *mihrab* arch,
Kaman Mosque, Rajasthan, late
12th century

FIG. 14

FIG. 14
Tomb of Hoshang Shah, Mandu,
Madhya Pradesh, c. 1440

FACING PAGE
FIG. 15
Jali window, tomb of Darya Khan,
Mandu, c. 1440

FIG. 16
Pierced dome of a bathhouse,
Mandu, 15th century

FIG. 16

FIG. 15

FIG. 17

Mandu in Madhya Pradesh became famous as the fifteenth–sixteenth-century capital of the Malwa kingdom under a dynasty which ruled between 1401 and 1531. Reaching its zenith under Hoshang Shah Ghuri (r. 1405–1435), the second Sultan of Malwa, the city was renamed 'Shadiabad' (City of Joy). The battlemented wall once enclosed tens of thousands of dwellings as well as lakes, marble palaces, mosques, gold-topped temples, and other buildings; however, few of those remain. Its many pleasure palaces, tombs and mosques are set amid gardens, pools and woodlands, while its ruins stretch for many miles along the crest of the mountains. Mandu's architecture had many features, including coloured tile-work, carved stucco and several types of *jali*s, of which a few impressive examples survive.

White marble *jali*s are to be found on Hoshang Shah's tomb (c. 1440), said to be the first marble building in India and a possible inspiration for Mughal tombs in the same material. The cuboid structure is entered through an arched opening flanked by two tall arched *jali* windows. These arches are matched on the opposite side by three further tall *jali*s (fig. 14) filling the interior with a grand play of filtered light. The *jali*s themselves are in the square grid formula popular in Gujarat, but integrate Islamicate geometrical motifs rather than sacred symbols of temple derivation.

A striking *jali* with bold floral lunette surmounting a geometric pattern is to be found on the tomb of Darya Khan, a nobleman employed at the royal court during the reign of Mahmud Shah II (1510–26).[24] The *jali* still bears traces of blue tile-work (fig. 15). Fine tracery work is also to be found in the arch heads of the Hindol Mahal, with several other buildings at Mandu also exhibiting this feature. An early-sixteenth century tomb pavilion known as the 'Jali Mahal' bears arches on all sides, three of which are completely closed in delicately pierced screens.[25]

A *hammam* at Mandu is a domed structure that shares its water supply with the Champa *baoli* (step-well). The ritual of bathing was popular in the Islamic and Indian worlds, involving the application of various unguents and perfumes as well as health-related procedures. The building had an elaborate hydraulic system capable of bringing cold and hot water to the interior, which was just one of many adept water management practices in Mandu's architecture. The bathhouse dome is pierced with stars and hexagons (fig. 16), which form both a symbolic heavenly canopy and a practical escape for the built-up steam. Such pierced *hammam* domes are also seen in the Ottoman world, where the openings are often covered with small glass vessels that allow in the light but protect from the elements.

Travelling north from Mandu, a dramatic surviving facade from the Jhanjiri Masjid (Lattice Mosque) at Jaunpur, Uttar Pradesh, offers a monumental sultanate *jali* from

FIG. 17
Jhanjiri Masjid, Jaunpur,
Uttar Pradesh, 1888,
British Library

FIG. 18
Jali at Chanderi dargah complex,
Madhya Pradesh, 15th century

FIG. 18

the world of the Sharqi rulers (fig. 17). The term *jhanjiri* refers to a perforated bamboo or reed screen and the name of the mosque is derived from a series of lattices in the screen over the main arch. Placed on a high mound, all that remains of the mosque is the central façade flanked by carved voussoirs and powerful inscriptions executed in relief; surrounding the main arch is the Throne Verse (*ayat al-qursi*) of the Qur'an and along the base appears a hadith of the Prophet recognizing the merit of those who build mosques.[26] The dynamic relation between areas of calligraphy, the letters of which are 1 foot and 4 inches high, and geometric *jali*s, both openwork and blind carved, is scaled accordingly to create an edifice of distinction. Sultan Ibrahim Sharqi (r. 1401–1440) built this mosque for Saint Saiyed Sadr i-Jahan Ajmali ('The Shining'). It was later attacked by Sikandar Lodi and its distinctive pink Chachakpur stone

FIG. 19

reused at other Jaunpur sites. Fine stone *jali*s, coloured tile-work and distinctive stone carving are also to be found in other monuments of Jaunpur's Sharqi era.

Sultanate architecture incorporated *jali* screens as a notable feature, reflecting foreign designs and motifs and also developing vibrant regional styles on the eve of Mughal rule. The central Indian area of Chanderi, conquered by the Mughal prince Babur in 1528, expresses the transition between these worlds. The evocative *jali*s of the Nizamuddin dargah complex at Chanderi (fig. 18) create the impression of an exquisite veil, soon to be lifted as the subcontinent entered the Mughal age. They feature square-based geometric grids executed in flat lines with highly dimensional floral medallions set into arches and spandrels, forming a distinctively local style with a touch of Mamluk influence.[27] At the Gwalior Fort in the same region, the structure and coloured tile decoration of the Man Mandir Palace had drawn the first Mughal emperor Babur's admiration. Built by the Tomara Rajput ruler Man Singh (r. 1486–1516), the eastern facade features cylindrical towers, domed pavilions and coloured tile-work decoration. Among the varieties of tiled designs on the upper levels of the exterior are plantain trees, pierced roundels and striding elephants in profile set against a pierced stone webbing to be seen against the sky (fig. 19).

FIG. 19
Man Mandir Palace, Gwalior,
Madhya Pradesh, early 16th century

FIG. 20
Wooden *jali* window,
Khanqah-i Maula mosque, Srinagar,
Jammu and Kashmir, 18th century

A transition of styles can also be seen in some of the features of Kashmiri Sultanate-era structures, rebuilt following fires that commonly occurred in the wooden architecture of this northernmost region of India. The Khanqah-i Maula mosque in Srinagar, first erected in the fourteenth century and rebuilt in the eighteenth century, was a centre of spiritual life in the valley and also a focal point for the artisan community and their crafts.[28] A wooden window on the second storey of

FIG. 20

the northern exterior (fig. 20) featuring medallion strapwork set around a gently cusping arch is among the decorative features that combine the local new and old styles. All these techniques and aesthetic effects were to further evolve into new expressions under Mughal patronage. ⊗

NOTES

1. Critchlow, *Islamic Patterns*, 57–73; Hillenbrand, *Islamic Architecture*, 455, fig 300.

2. Ruggles, "Making Vision Manifest," 131–156.

3. 'Nur: Light in Art and Science from the Islamic World,' travelling exhibition, Seville, Oct. 2013–Feb. 2014, and Dallas, Mar. 2014–June 2014.

4. Hillenbrand, *Islamic Architecture*, 89–92.

5. Saba (curator), 'Pattern, Color, Light,' July 2015–Jan. 2016.

6. Image archives include The David Wade Archive; The Creswell Archive.

7. Grabar, *Mediation of Ornament*, 1992.

8. Necipoğlu and Payne, *Histories of Ornament*, 2016.

9. Flood, "Flaw in the Carpet", 93.

10. Necipoğlu, *The Topkapi Scroll*, 1995.

11. Abbas, "Ornamental Jalis of Mughals," 135–147.

12. Dodds, *Al-Andalus: Art of Islamic Spain*, 252.

13. Flood, "Earliest Islamic Windows," 67–89; Flood, "Ottoman Windows," 431–463.

14. Creswell, *Early Muslim Architecture*, 135–149.

15. Thanks are due to William Dalrymple for pointing out this rose window.

16. Williams, "Reflections of Reality," 228–29.

17. Greenwood and de Guise, *Inspired by the East*, 2019.

18. Thanks are due to Martina Rugiadi for this reference.

19. Flood, "Before the Mughals," 1–39.

20. Bloom, "Marble Panels in Mosque of Kairouan," 2017.

21. Sharma, "A Cross-cultural Dialogue," 249–62. Accessed April 1, 2020.

22. Thanks are due to Mitchell Crites for this observation.

23. Shokoohy and Shokoohy, "Architecture of Baha Al-Din Tughrul," 114–132.

24. Yazdani, *Mandu: City of Joy*, 102–103.

25. Ibid., 121–124.

26. Fasih ud-din, *Sharqi Monuments of Jaunpur*, 25.

27. Digby, "Before Timur Came," 298–356, 312–13, describes the "severely controlled lattices" and other ornamental features as having Mamluk influence.

28. Hamdani, "Kashmir's Islamic Religious Architecture," 12–14, 41.

Divine Order
Early Mughal Visions

*"In comparison to the light of your cheek, the solar disc
is as dim as a candle in the sun."*[1]

Amir Khusrau, d. 1325

With the establishment of Mughal rule in the early sixteenth century, a new era dawned in the development of art and architecture in the Indian subcontinent. As ambitious and creative patrons, Mughal rulers employed numerous talents and integrated regional and historical styles from around the burgeoning empire. The resulting idioms shaped the aesthetics of South Asia for many centuries. Much of the splendour of Mughal buildings lies in their elaborate decoration, harmonizing patterns and motifs in stone carving and inlay, wall painting, carved stucco, and perforated *jali* screens.[2] The latter came into their own as a characteristic feature in Sufi shrines and also royal tombs, reflecting the close spiritual links between rulers and Sufi orders as key to the evolution of Mughal aesthetics. *Jali* screens and walls at Sufi shrines played an important role for pilgrims who came from all sections of society, Hindu and Muslim alike. Visitors performed the practice of tying *niyat* threads (prayer intentions) on *jali*s (fig. 3) as a way of seeking blessings and paying homage, a ritual that survives to the present day. In this shared practice, the *jali*s of Sufi shrines became meeting points of spiritual encounter between different communities. Royal tombs functioned in a related mode, memorializing the interred ruler or royal figures while inviting visitation, engagement and counterpart aesthetic experiences.

FACING PAGE
Tomb of Sheikh Salim
Chishti, Fatehpur Sikri,
Uttar Pradesh, 1581

FIG. 1

FIG. 2

FIG. 1
Kaanch Mahal, Sikandra,
Uttar Pradesh, early 17th century

FIG. 2
Conversation in a lattice balcony,
detail from the *Wedding of
Siyavush and Farangis*, folio from
the Shahnama of Shah Tahmasp,
attributed to Qasim ibn 'Ali Tabriz,
Iran, c. 1525–30
Gift of Arthur A. Houghton Jr., 1970,
The Metropolitan Museum of Art
1970.301.28

*Jali*s in early Mughal buildings expanded the geometric ornament of the preceding Sultanate- and Sur-era buildings, with a greater feeling for lightness and decorative refinement. *Jali*s grew larger in size and yet more delicate in presence, forming walls of filtered light that had changing visual impact through the day and the seasons. White marble (*sang-i marmar*) became a prominent material as the Makrana quarry provided stone for ongoing building projects. New artistic idioms spurred craftsmen and designers to create complex geometrical designs in two and three dimensions. As *jali* strapwork in stone became lighter and airier, it required greater technical prowess to carve away larger amounts of the material. *Jali*s appeared in all kinds of formal and informal contexts, often translating wooden structures into stone, such as the charming balconies in the early seventeenth-century Kaanch Mahal (figs 1, 2).

However, early Mughal *jali*s were not exclusively geometric in their patterns. One of the greatest vine carvings is from the tomb of Muhammad Ghaus, built in this same period, the flowing leaves, however, flattened and following an ordered symmetry within a rectangular border (see figs 31–33). Naturalistic hints seen in ribbing and texture anticipate the transformation of the lines of the *jali* into fully three-dimensional vines that was to follow in later buildings. Other examples of organic or curving *jali* carvings can be seen in foliate arabesques and ribbon cloud-bands, often found in the spandrels of arched geometrical screens.

Allegories of Light in the Mughal Arts

The Mughals developed a system of symbolism and allegory in their arts, fashioning a complex and multi-layered visual language that drew on Indian, Islamic and European sources to create powerful new idioms. The metaphorical use of light and radiance appears in many guises in Mughal art, expressing themes of divine kingship and spiritual illumination. The Rajput houses—with which the Mughals were matrimonially and politically joined—also shared notions of solar and lunar descent in their royal lineages (*suryavanshi* and *chandravanshi*). Other sources for this leitmotif included ancient Indian traditions of sun worship and notions of divine kingship, and the ancient Persian concept of divine glory (*farr-i izadi*).

Solar and lunar symbols pervade Mughal royal imagery and emblems of state and courtly practices, many of which are described in the *'Ain-i Akbari*, or Annals of Emperor Akbar (r. 1556–1605). These came to include a style of throne surmounted by a solar umbrella (*chhatri*) with sun rays represented in the pearl fringes; a rounded royal sunshade (*aftabgir*); the state flag with the symbol of a sun behind a feline (*shir-u khurshid*); royal canopies embellished with the motif of a solar disc flanked by birds-of-paradise; and solar and lunar weighing ceremonies.

Emperor Jahangir (r. 1605–27) was particularly interested in symbols that conveyed a sense of radiance and luminescence.[3] This can be seen in his title of Nur al-Din (Light of Religion) and that of his wife, empress Nur Jahan (Light of the World). Coinage issued by them—the *sikka-i nur*—also included the term *nur*, or light. Jahangir's painters frequently represented him with a single or double halo, incorporating both a solar disc and lunar crescent. Light came to pervade Mughal courtly objects too. A taste for translucent and precious materials such as jade, marble, rock-crystal and gemstones including red spinel, described in Persian sources as light (*la'l*), became part of the Mughal aesthetic.

The awareness of the metaphorical potential of light and darkness is no less apparent in architecture, seen in the conceptualization of shrines, tombs and garden settings in which bright, translucent and reflective materials, relief carving, stone inlay and perforated screens play an important role in amplifying heavenly and celestial themes. In tombs, light was made to filter through *jali* walls to surround grave markers and cenotaphs, such as in the starry marble mesh that surrounds the interior structure at the shrine of the saint Sheikh Salim Chishti at Fatehpur Sikri (see fig. 15). The resting place of royal figures also echoed this idea. At the tomb of Emperor Humayun (r. 1530–40; 1555–56) in Delhi geometric *jali* screens dapple light around the inner chamber and in the surrounding vestibules. Mughal painters often depicted their royal patrons at *jharokha* windows surrounded by lattice screens.

❖ Royal Patronage

The brief Sur era (1540–55), which intervened during Humayun's reign, saw several important buildings with styles of decoration that likely provided inspiration for Mughal architectural ornament. Located in the Purana Qila complex in Delhi, the fine ornamentation of the five-bay Qila-i Kuhna mosque built by Sher Shah Suri in 1541 includes epigraphy and intricate geometric patterns in coloured stone inlay. Sur-period *jali*s are to be found in the architectural remains at Narnaul. These appear (somewhat restored) in the handsomely decorated grey-and-red tomb of Ibrahim Khan Sur at Narnaul (d. 1518), built over his grave by his grandson Sher Shah. Comparable *jali*s can be found in the octagonal tomb of Isa Khan, built in 1547 in Delhi. The *jali*s of these two tombs resemble each other, with a distinctive square-rectangle body surmounted by an openwork arched border, demonstrating a unified style of the Lodi-Sur periods, quite distinct from Mughal developments that followed.[4]

The ancient Muslim neighbourhood of Nizamuddin in Delhi grew around the tomb and shrine of the Sufi saint Hazrat Nizamuddin Auliya (1236–1325)

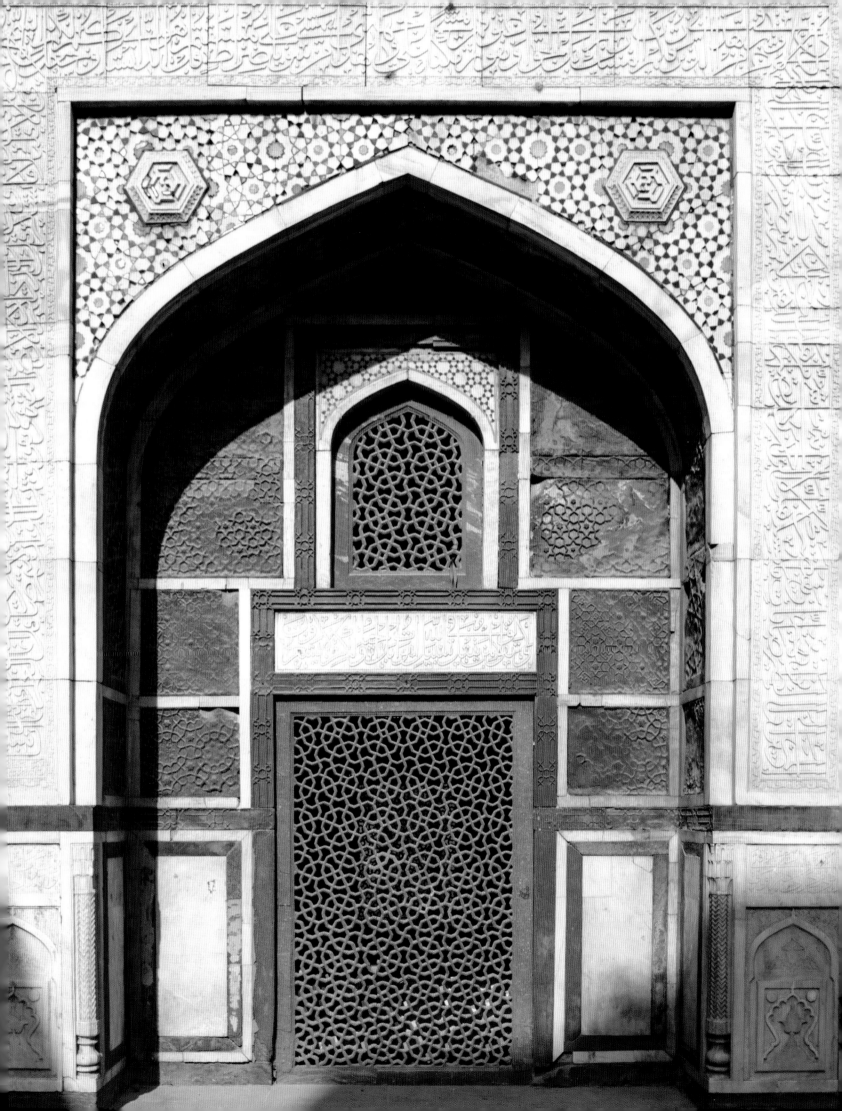

FIG. 5

FIG. 5
Chaunsath Khambha, Delhi, 1623–24

and encompasses many richly ornamented historical buildings. The tomb of Nizamuddin itself has been rebuilt several times. The present structure is based on the edifice completed during the reign of Emperor Akbar in 1562, but it has been renovated and embellished repeatedly. Among the Mughal additions at the site are handsome and protective low *jali* walls around the shrine of the Sufi saint and the adjoining grave (*mazar*) of the mystic poet and Akbar's courtier Amir Khusrau (1253–1325), some of them adorned with carved relief verses running along the edge.

The tombs of Ataga Khan, who served at Akbar's court, and that of his son Mirza Aziz Kokaltash also lie within the Nizamuddin complex.[5] Ataga Khan's tomb, a small cuboid structure completed in 1566–67, displays facades of great distinction with fine calligraphy and geometric designs (fig. 4), including Timurid tile mosaic patterns interpreted in stone intarsia. Overlapping circles decorate the surface, seamlessly continuing from open-work *jali* to carved relief. Nearby lies Mirza 'Aziz's tomb (1623–24), better known as 'Chaunsath Khambha' (64 Columns), its central hypostyle structure surrounded with square-grid white marble latticework (fig. 5).

FIGs 6 & 7 (FACING PAGE)
Mihrab jali and detail, Humayun's Tomb, Delhi, 1572

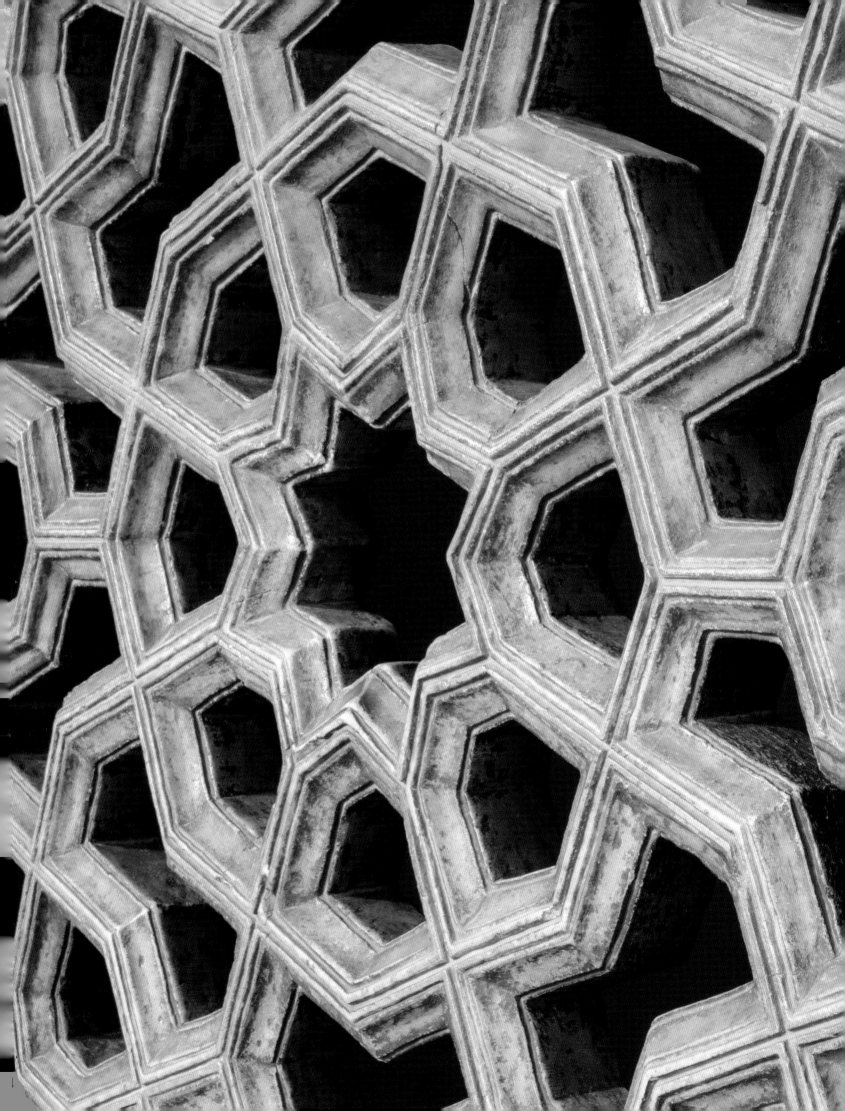

All throughout the complex are *jali* screens and railings of various geometric designs, some made of marble and others of painted sandstone. The embellishment of such railings was mentioned by Jahangir on several occasions. In his eighth regnal year (1613–14), the emperor had ordered silver cladding to be applied to wooden railings in the redecoration of the Diwan-i Khas in Agra for a "different splendor and look".[6] The shrine of Sheikh Mu'inuddin Chishti at Ajmer was furnished with golden railings in July 1616: "For the outcome of several things I made a vow to have a gold lattice work railing installed around Khwaja's tomb. It was completed on the twenty-seventh of the month. I ordered a screen installed. It cost one hundred ten thousand rupees."[7]

The mausoleum of Emperor Humayun, completed by his son Akbar in 1572, is seen as a landmark in the establishment of the imperial style. Attributed to the Persian architect-and-poet duo of father and son Mirak Mirza Ghiyas and Sayyid Muhammad, the tomb's symmetrical floor plan and elevation are matched by formal schemes of openings and axial placement of sandstone and marble screens, their materials carefully chosen to create dynamic contrasts of colour and texture on each facet. In the main chamber, the *qibla* wall is indicated by a marble *jali* of star-and-hexagon design into which the *mihrab* arch has been inscribed (fig. 6). The grooving and bevelling of the straps result in almost five levels of depth, while the edging of chevrons adds an ornamental delicacy (fig. 7). Smaller sandstone *jalis* in adjoining chambers along the *qibla* wall echo the same *mihrab* formula. This design, in which the *mihrab* glows against filtered light replacing the words of Sura 24, provoked the Mughal courtier Badauni to observe that its purpose was to allow the cleansing rays of the morning sun to fall on the face of the interred.[8] The prominent six-pointed stars that appear in the *jalis*, around the drum of the dome of the mausoleum and as motifs in the arch spandrels, can be interpreted as allusions to Humayun's strong interest in astronomical observation and celestial symbols.[9]

The palatial city complex of Fatehpur Sikri built by Akbar in 1572 ushered in new visions of space, view, framing devices, vista and ornament. Its palace buildings have been studied and appreciated from almost every point of view, except perhaps their elegant *jalis* that are present among all the other fine decoration. One discrete style is that of a rectangular window with a fine geometric grid of octagons and intersecting straps set into rather plain walls of red sandstone, as seen in the so-called Khas Mahal (fig. 8). The artist Farrukh Beg includes this feature in the upper balcony of a building, rendering a similar design in the *Baburnama* (memoirs of Emperor Babur) (fig. 9). However, photographic evidence from the nineteenth century shows that some of the *jali* windows and railings in

FIG. 9

FACING PAGE
FIG. 8
Khas Mahal, Fatehpur Sikri,
Uttar Pradesh, late 16th century

FIG. 9
Babur Entertains in Sultan Ibrahim Lodi's Palace, detached folio from a dispersed copy of a *Baburnama*, by Farrukh Beg, c. 1585
Arthur M. Sackler Gallery, S1986.232

FIG. 10

FIG. 10
Akbar inspects the construction
at Fatehpur Sikri, folio from the
Akbarnama, by Tulsi, Bandi and
Madhav Khord, c. 1590–95
Collection of Victoria and Albert
Museum

FIGs 11 & 12
Sandstone *jali*s, 16th century
The Metropolitan Museum of Art,
Rogers Fund, 1993, 1993.67.1 and
1993.67.2

FIG. 11

FIG. 12

the Khas Mahal are replacements, very well executed nevertheless.[10] Another of the Sikri *jali* styles is that of broad rectangular screens composed of overlapping circles.[11] This type appears in a folio of the *Akbarnama* ('Book of Akbar' by his court historian and biographer Abu'l-Fazl) illustrating the building of the city where Akbar reviews the work of a stone-cutter (fig. 10). A pair of similar screens in the Metropolitan Museum of Art incorporate sacred symbols such as a meander (swastika), lotus (*padma*) or wheel (*chakra*) woven into the pattern (figs 11, 12). Other sandstone *jali*s in Fatehpur Sikri introduce polygonal and grid designs (figs 13, 14).

The white marble tomb of the Sufi saint Sheikh Salim Chishti at Fatehpur Sikri, dated to 1580–81, can be considered an apogee of the art of the *jali*, both for the quality of the individual screens and also for the mystical and theatrical effect they lend to the space as a whole. Here, a small sandstone site of homage to the

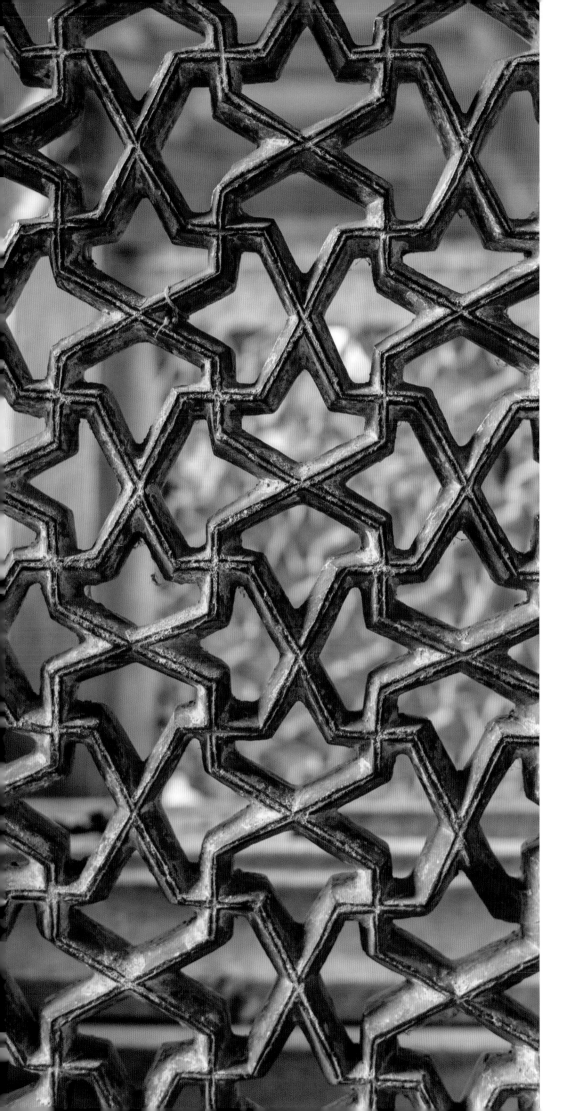

FIG. 13
Jali wall with polygonal pattern
surrounding grave markers,
Fatehpur Sikri, Uttar Pradesh,
late 16th century

FACING PAGE
FIG. 14
Sandstone *jali*s in circular design,
Fatehpur Sikri, late 16th century

FIG. 15

saintly figure was later enclosed in an exquisite marble filigree (fig. 15) web. This luminous creation has captured the eyes of painters and photographers, including the American orientalist Edwin Lord Weeks who recorded the locale in 1883 (fig. 16). The style and proportions of the white marble *jali* galleries that enclose the inner sepulchre express a stylistic debt to Gujarat. The fine marble webbing extends into serpentine struts (fig. 17) that support the overhanging ledge surmounting the entrance porch and structure (fig. 18), another feature associated with Gujarat. Jahangir ascribes the remarkable screens to the commission of Qutbuddin Khan Kukaltash, believed to be either the grandson of Sheikh Salim Chishti or another nobleman of the same name who supported the building of the adjoining Jama Masjid[12]: "One of the greatest monuments built during His Majesty Arsh-Ashyani's reign is this tomb mosque. Without exaggeration, it is a really superb building. There may not be anything like it anywhere. The building is all of very pure stone, and five lacs of rupees from the imperial treasury were spent on it. The cost of the screen around the tomb, the paving under the dome and the frontal arch of the mosque that Qutbuddin Khan Kukaltash provided in marble is over and above that amount."[13]

FIG. 16

FIGs 15 (FACING PAGE) & 17
Tomb of Sheikh Salim Chishti,
Fatehpur Sikri, Uttar Pradesh, 1581

FIG. 16
*White marble tomb at Fatehpur
Sikri* by Edwin Lord Weeks, 1883

FOLLOWING PAGES
FIG. 18
Jali wall, Tomb of Sheikh Salim
Chishti, 1581

FIG. 17

A dazzling play of ornament is seen at Akbar's tomb at Sikandra, completed in 1613. The bold and spectacular inlaid patterns of gateways and walls are echoed in the *jali*s that abut them. Where inlay and carving creates dynamic decoration, the *jali* adds dimension and framework, on a large scale, particularly around the entrances into the main tomb. The top terrace of the tomb contains a marble cenotaph under open skies, surrounded by a vibrant gallery of geometric *jali* walls (fig. 19). Singular floral motifs carved on Akbar's cenotaph introduce natural forms into the ornamental language of the terrace setting. The rhythms of arabesque borders and geometric *jali*s, together with the naturalistically carved motifs, bring together the emerging styles of the Jahangir period. This magnificent resting place built by Jahangir for his father includes a seven-*jali* wall along the access route (fig. 20), which would have provided a private approach for royal visitors. These seven *jali* screens incorporate geometricized designs in the main areas,

PREVIOUS PAGES
FIG. 19
Akbar's cenotaph on the *jali* terrace, Sikandra, Uttar Pradesh, 1613

FIG. 20 (BELOW)
Seven-*jali* wall, tomb of Akbar, Sikandra, 1613

including star patterns and zigzag lines that contrast with 'chinoiserie' spandrels containing cloud-bands and lotuses and split palm leaf designs (*islimi-khatai*) of Timurid inspiration.

Nur Jahan (1577–1645), Jahangir's dynamic last queen, had a powerful impact on the aesthetics of the seventeenth century. Among her architectural commissions is the tomb built for her parents Itimad ud-Daulah and Azmat Begum at Agra (completed 1628) that introduced many important ornamental features, including wall painting, a style of coloured stone inlay considered to be the precursor to the *pietra dura* inlay of the Taj Mahal and spectacular *jali*s. These are found on the upper level of the tomb in a central pavilion which is surmounted by a low, elongated dome emulating a style of wooden covering used by Sufis. The dome rests on a structure of exquisitely carved *jali* walls (fig. 21), which have a particularly mesmerizing effect

FOLLOWING PAGES
FIG. 21
Tomb of Itimad ud-Daulah,
Agra, Uttar Pradesh, 1628

FIG. 22

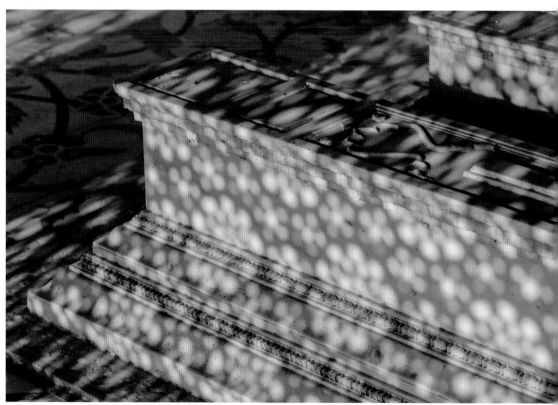

FIGs 22, 23 & 24 (FACING PAGE)
Dappled views and *jali* screen,
tomb of Itimad ud-Daulah,
Agra, Uttar Pradesh, 1628

FIG. 23

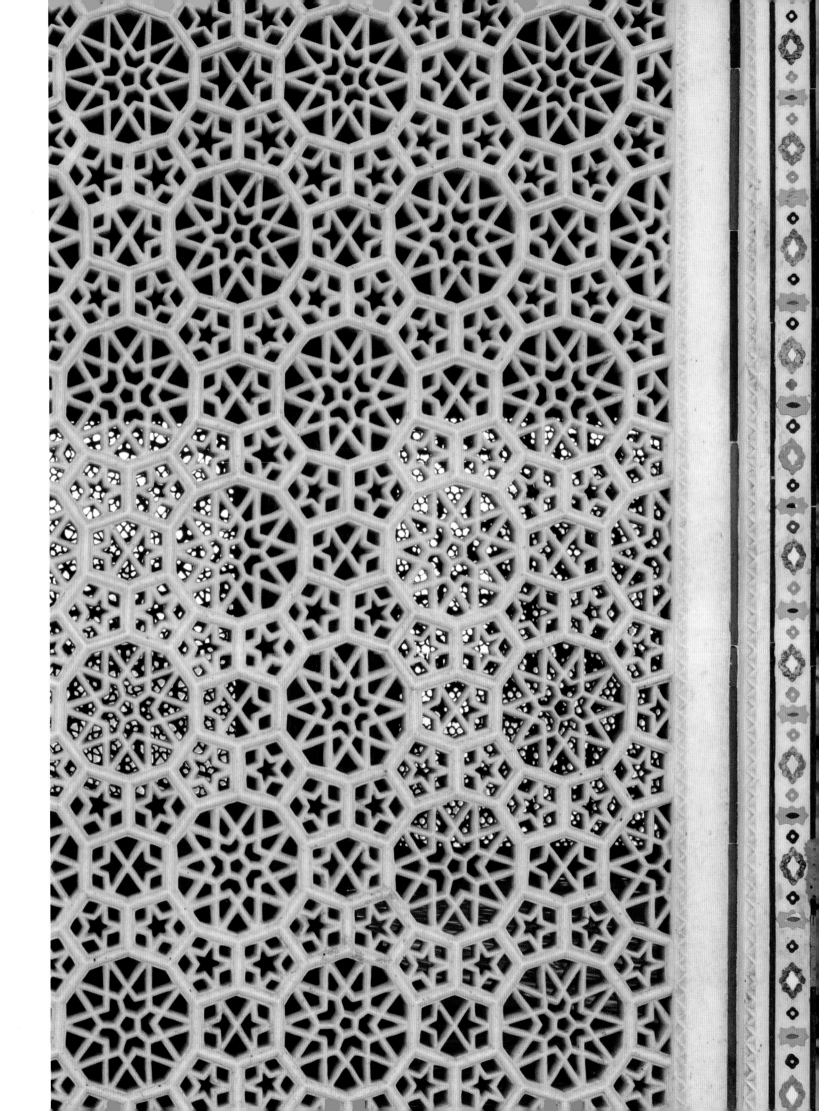

FIG. 25

FIG. 26a

FIG. 26b

FIG. 27

when viewed from within the interior chamber. They push away the world but bring in the light, which casts dappled shadows over the central cenotaphs and a bold arabesque inlaid floor (figs 22, 23 & 24). The effect of these walls upon the cenotaphs is to lift them into a celestial orbit in contrast with the actual location of the graves in the dark tomb chamber underground. With its four-sided transparency and elevation into the light from all directions, this space can be seen as one that realizes the full potential of filtered light. Distinctive *jali*s with zigzag parallel lines are found in the lower level of the main building (fig. 25). A pair of such *jali*s in greyish marble are in a private collection (figs 26a, 26b) while another single *jali* is in the Metropolitan Museum of Art (fig. 27).

Exceptional *jali*s of celestial design can be found in the beautifully ornamented tomb of Shah Pir in Meerut (fig. 28), reportedly built in the early 1600s and associated with Nur Jahan's patronage. Shah Pir had earlier attached himself to Jahangir and received support from the emperor for the construction of a mosque in Meerut in 1613.[14] The Pir's tomb itself lies in an unfinished and partly ruined state without a dome, leaving

FIG. 25
Exterior wall with stone inlay and *jali* screens, tomb of Itimad ud-Daulah, Agra, Uttar Pradesh, 1628

FIG. 26a and 26b
Pair of *jali*s with zigzag lines, c. 1700 Private collection, New York

FIG. 27
Zigzag *jali* with two geometric designs, one within the other, early 17th century The Metropolitan Museum of Art, Rogers Fund, 1984, 1984.193

FOLLOWING PAGES
FIG. 28
Tomb of Shah Pir, Meerut, Uttar Pradesh, early 17th century

FIG. 30

his grave exposed to the sky and allowing light to flood into the interior. The red sandstone structure contains well-articulated arched recesses on both its exterior and interior walls. Floral vases and arabesques offset the recesses which are filled with diverse *jali*-like geometric patterns in intricately worked shallow relief, realized as perforated windows (fig. 29) at both levels in the middle of each side. Varieties of arch and niche designs echo one another's forms and enclose interlaced stars and hexagons, arabesques, and floral vases—the latter were to find great favour in the architectural ornament of Shah Jahani buildings.

FACING PAGE
FIG. 29
Window of interlaced stars and hexagons *jali* at the tomb of Shah Pir, Meerut, Uttar Pradesh, early 17th century

FIG. 30
Jali crenellations with reciprocal design, tomb of Sheikh Phul, Bayana, Rajasthan, 16th century

FIG. 31

In the city of Gwalior, the monumental tomb of the saint Muhammad Ghaus (d. 1653) represents a high point in the art of the *jali*. The Sufi brothers Muhammad Ghaus and Sheikh Phul (Bahlul, d. 1539) were significant figures in the circle of Humayun, bringing esoteric Shattari dimensions of astronomy, astrology and alchemy to the royal court. Humayun's well-documented interests in these areas were demonstrated in courtly practices such as courtiers dressing according to assigned planetary colours and sitting in circular spaces relating to astrological symbols.[15] Sheikh Phul was attributed with all kinds of magical powers by Mughal chroniclers who noted his influence over the emperor.[16] The small and evocative tomb of the

Sheikh stands among rugged hills in Bayana—a stark white *ivan* arch surmounted by a line of *jali* crenellations (fig. 30).[17] This frieze of opposing and undulating blossoms is similar to the reciprocal designs found among the more lavish *jali*s in the tomb of his younger brother Muhammad Ghaus.

Muhammad Ghaus was responsible for the translation of several yogic texts, including the *Amritkunda* as the *Bahr al-Hayat* (Ocean of Life), and described his spiritual experience of ascension in the *Jawahir-i Khamsa* (Five Jewels). No wonder then that his tomb in Gwalior (figs 31, 32), built in 1565 under Akbar, stands out

FIG. 31, FIG. 32 (FOLLOWING PAGES) & FIG. 33
Jali walls, tomb of Muhammad Ghaus, Gwalior, Madhya Pradesh, c. 1565

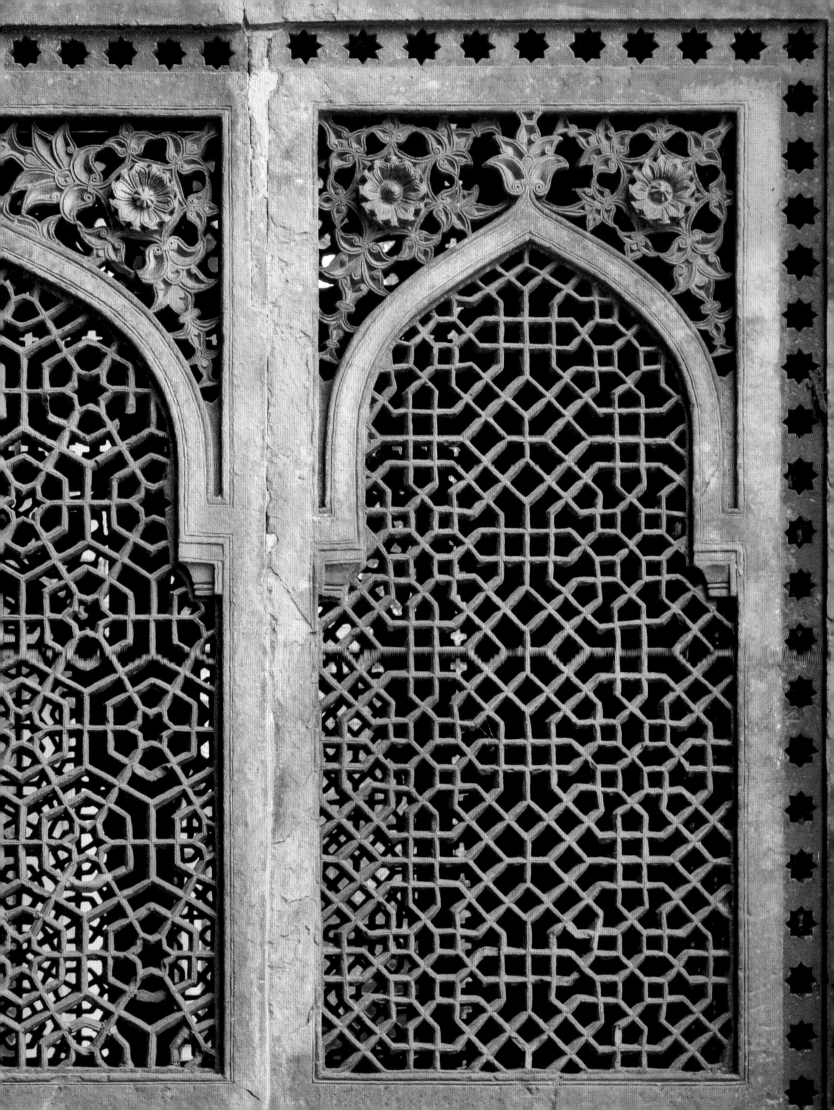

FIG. 33

for its language of filtered light and ethereality and its allusions to the mystical and yogic worlds. The tomb is a square stone building with a large central dome and hexagonal corner towers crowned by pavilions (*chhatris*). The basic octagonal pattern of the tomb of Humayun built two years later is regarded as a simplification of this mausoleum's floor plan. Perforated marble screens form an exterior *jali* wall of luminous geometric grids around the verandah surrounding the tomb's central chamber. Projecting chambers with tall arches contain impressive lattice screens of stylized vegetal design such as organic vines and leafy grids. The formula brings together celestial symbols of Shattari metaphysics with metaphors of natural order in a way that captures the blending of philosophical traditions that Muhammad Ghaus was identified with. Within the inner chamber the *jali* style continues; the saint's cenotaph is a central structure surrounded by *jali* walls (fig. 33) which are surmounted by an elongated dome. The courtyard of the tomb of Muhammad Ghaus contains the memorial of Mian Tansen, court vocalist of Akbar and one of the 'nine gems' of the Mughal court. This structure has open walls with low *jali* railings. Tansen (d. 1586), who was born in Gwalior, is said to have been a devotee of Muhammad Ghaus.[18] Together, these tombs form important landmarks in the history and personalities of the Mughal sphere. ⊗

NOTES

1. Thackston, "Light in Persian Poetry," 194.

2. Michell, *Majesty of Mughal Decoration*, 2007.

3. Stronge, S, "By the Light of the Sun of Jahangir", 2015.

4. Jain, "Structure as a document,", 2008.

5. Welch, "The Emperor's Grief," 255–73.

6. Thackston, *The Jahangirnama*, 145.

7. Ibid., 225.

8. Lowry, "Humayn's Tomb," 133–148.

9. Ibid., 144.

10. Thanks are due to Dr Gursharan Sidhu for sharing a photograph by Samuel Bourne of the site which shows broken *jali*s.

11. Creswell, *Early Muslim Architecture: Vol. 1*, 75–79; Bonner, *Islamic Geometric Patterns*, 14. Perhaps some remote idea from the early Umayyad axial grid windows provided inspiration for the dynamic new projects of a burgeoning Mughal style.

12. Thackston, *Jahangirnama*, 294. Rizvi, *Fatehpur Sikri*, 76–77, gives the date 1580–81 and suggests the screens are made in 1606; Smith, *Fatehpur-Sikri*, 11, pl. XVII, gives the date 979/1571 over the entrance to the inner tomb chamber; Koch, "Influence on Mughal Architecture," 168–69, suggests however that Qutb al-din Khan could have been the brother of Akbar's foster-father Shams al-Din Khan, who had a connection to Gujarat and who also paid for the marble floor of the *mihrab* chamber and the great *pishtāq* of the Jami mosque in the courtyard of which the tomb stands. ARCHNET NEXT, https://archnet. org/sites/2657, suggests the screens are Jahangir period in style.

13. Thackston, *Jahangirnama*, 294.

14. ibid., 145.

15. Lowry, "Humayun's Tomb," 143.

16. Alam, "Mughals, Sufi Shaikhs and Akbari Dispensation," 135–74.

17. Khan, "Two Early Timurid Monuments of Bayana," 297–306. Sheikh Phul's building was visited by Jahangir in 1617–18.

18. Wade, *Imaging Sound*, 113–15.

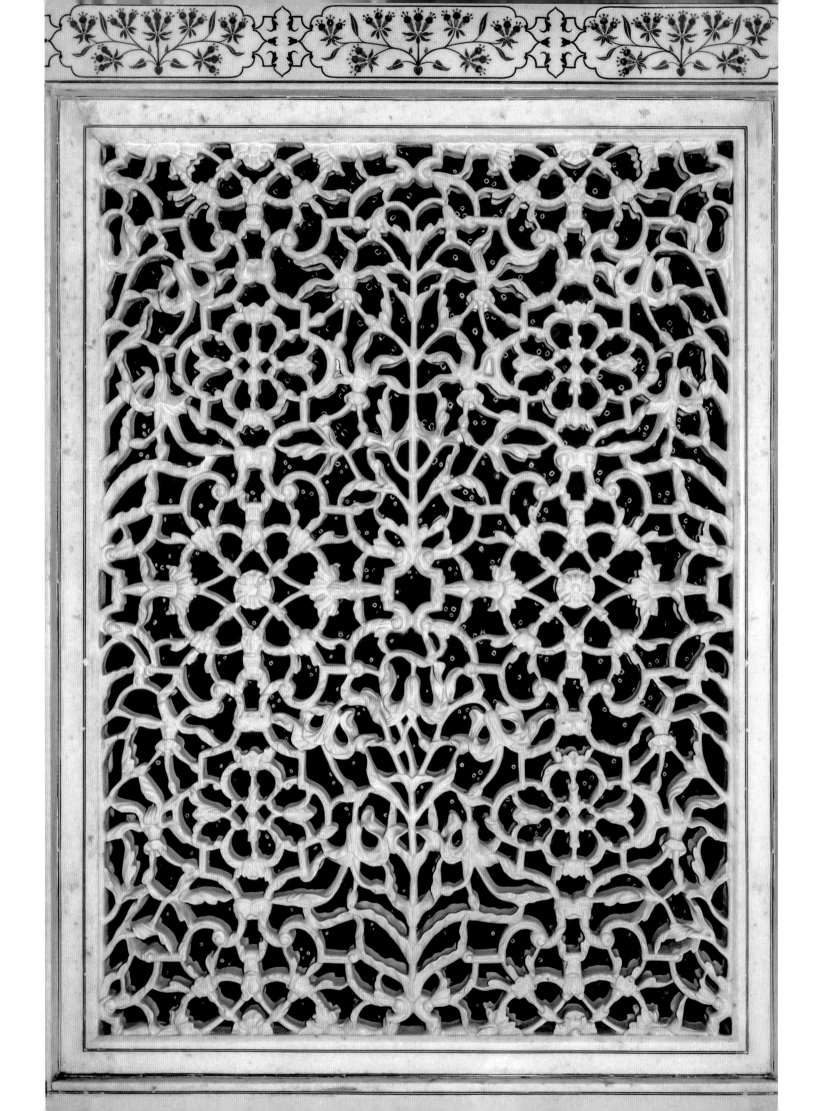

The Flower Philosophy of Shah Jahan Expressed in the Art of the *Jali*

Ebba Koch

The art of the Mughal *jali* underwent a dramatic change under Shah Jahan (r. 1628–58): like all Shah Jahani ornament it became floral. The new floral aesthetic affected all art forms and objects of court life, but it was in the buildings of the emperor that it was exhibited most prominently and for a broader audience to see. This new approach has to be placed in a wider context: by the seventeenth century a predominantly floral decorative vocabulary had established itself as mainstream ornament in the arts of the three great empires of the Islamic world, the Ottomans, the Safavids, and the Mughals.[1] Flower and plant decoration took the place of the previously favoured geometrical and arabesque patterns still considered by many as 'typically Islamic'; these continued however to be used, as a sideline. What sets the Shah Jahani floral trend apart from related trends elsewhere is its revolutionary naturalism, and that flower and plant ornament became a programmatic expression of the emperor's ruling philosophy of a sun king who generates bloom in his empire.

Naturalistic ornament brought a long involvement of the Mughals with plants and their representation to its artistic apogee.[2] For models of naturalism, the Mughals turned to the arts of Europe; they based their studies of flowers and plants, including those which were native to their own environment, on the illustrations in scientific European herbals.[3] These works were printed in Antwerp by Christophe Plantin, who had also published the famous *Polyglot Bible* (1568–72) which the first Jesuit Mission had brought to the court of Akbar in 1580.[4] The flower studies of the painters of the court atelier were transferred by Shah Jahan's stone carvers to marble and sandstone relief, *munabbat kari*. The carving was in deeply undercut relief with close attention to detail, transferring the naturalism of the European source to the marble surface. Even more naturalistic effects could be obtained with flowers and plants inlaid with semi-precious stones, a technique which the Mughals adapted from Florentine *comesso di pietre dure* or *pietra dura*. They knew it from European artists who came to the Mughal court, and from Italian works which

FACING PAGE
Marble lacework
screen from the
Taj Mahal cenotaph
wall, Agra, Uttar
Pradesh, 1643

visitors brought as presents for the emperor. The Mughals called the technique *parchin kari*. The poet Abu Talib Kalim Kashani tells us that the painterly effects that could be obtained with *parchin kari* made it possible to create the desired naturalistic flowers, permanent, and superior to their counterparts in nature:

"They have inlaid flowers of stone in the marble,
What they lack in smell they make up with colour."[5]

In the medium of the *jali*—the Sanskrit-derived Hindi term for perforated stone screens, naturalism as the strived-for ideal was transposed into a different sphere: on the one hand the plant forms acquired a third dimension, and on the other, their matter—the stone—was dematerialized and became transcendent. The process was anticipated in the splendid *jali* windows of the mosque of Sidi Sayyid at Ahmedabad, Gujarat (1572–73), where trees with undulating branches and tendrils generate a dense and complex floral pattern covering the whole arched surface (see 'Sacred Symbols', fig. 26).[6] Shah Jahan must have seen and admired these windows when as a prince he was governor of Gujarat (1618–22) and had a garden palace at Ahmedabad.

In floral *jalis* made for Shah Jahan's buildings we can observe a chronological sequence in which the naturalistic form is eventually dissolved in floating organic arabesques and trellises. Three outstanding examples demonstrate this process. The most naturalistic and probably earliest floral *jalis* are those of the lunettes above the doors of the Shah Burj, the imperial tower pavilion of the Agra Fort, of the early 1630s. A pointed arch is divided into four compartments in which are set a group of plants in a mirror symmetrical arrangement, a formal principle dear to the designers of Shah Jahan (see 'Heavenly Gardens', fig. 15). In the lower central field, we can identify a group of three irises, related in their botanical style to those individual flowering plants which appear in marble relief on the dadoes of this and other palace buildings of the fort and on the dadoes of the Taj Mahal, completed in 1643. The Shah Burj irises are flanked by less specific flowering bushes, and on top is a leafy plant.

A distinct dematerialization occurs in the five windows of the Diwan-i Khas, the Hall of Private Audience, also in the Agra Fort and datable somewhat later in the 1630s. In each arched window is set a vase with flowers in a symmetrical arrangement (see 'Heavenly Gardens', fig. 8). Similar vases appear at the same time in marble relief on the dadoes of the central tomb chamber of the Taj Mahal. Like the individual flowering plants, they are derived from European models.[7] What is not European at all is their dissolution into openwork in the windows of the Diwan-i Khas, to the extent that the form of the vase, with a central iris flanked by martagon lilies and narcissus-like flowers (shaped like pinwheels), can be perceived only after close scrutiny.

In the great enclosure around the cenotaphs of Mumtaz Mahal and Shah Jahan in the Taj Mahal, Mughal *jali* art reached its apogee. The octagonal marble screen, called *mahjar-i musamman-i mushabbak* by Shah Jahan's historian 'Abd al-Hamid Lahauri, was put up in 1643 to replace a screen of enamelled gold.[8] Its *jali* panels are set in frames inlaid with botanically identifiable flowers and plant ornaments in semi-precious stone—*parchin kari*. In the screens, the natural flower form is transformed in the artistic medium of open stonework, where it becomes abstract: two pseudo-botanical stems with hanging blossoms resembling martagon lilies are placed one above the other and constitute the central axis of a vegetal scroll system which generates symmetrically arranged cartouches and medallions (see 'Heavenly Gardens', fig. 1). The whole combines the diaphanous ethereal character of the *jali* with the sculptural dynamic of three-dimensionally interlocking and intertwining forms. The dialectic potential of the *jali* to dissolve matter and at the same time express recognizable shape is explored to its fullest. An even greater abstraction sets in in the famous but sadly damaged 'Scales of Justice' screen in the Delhi Red Fort (see 'Heavenly Gardens', fig. 4), completed 1648, where candelabras of stylized lilies are integrated into a vegetal trellis pattern connected with little cartouches filled, in turn, with a net of miniature geometric trellises.

The extraordinary skill in overcoming matter physically and conceptually with these transparent amalgamations of figural and non-figural designs creates wonder and surprise at the artistic energies available at the emperor's command. The creation of flowers and plants in multiple media and all types of architectural ornament had a distinct symbolic purpose. In the funerary context of the Taj Mahal, it was, as the poets tell us, to create for the emperor's deceased queen Mumtaz Mahal in the material world here on earth a garden-house with ever-blooming flowers which, in an inverted Platonic sense, would ensure for her a paradisiacal counter image in the Unseen World.[9]

In the emperor's palaces, plant ornament also evoked paradisical associations, but there it served a political purpose—to express his cosmic power as a sun king. The poets celebrate Shah Jahan as sun of the empire, as earthly counterpart of the heavenly planet: he is *inter alia* 'the sun (*aftab*) of the sky of world rulership (*sipihr-i jahandari*)'.[10] The concept is architecturally realized by what I have described previously as the 'vegetabilization programme' of Shah Jahan's palaces.[11] The message is ingeniously epitomized in the ornamentation of the twin baldachins of the south wing of the so-called Machchhi Bhawan, a palatial courtyard in the

FIG. 1

FIG. 2

FIG. 1
Dome lined with a *jali*-like trellis pattern radiating from a sun in the centre, of the front baldachin in the south wing of the so-called Machchhi Bhawan in the Agra Fort, of the 1630s. This projecting baldachin housed the golden throne of Shah Jahan.

FIG. 2
Dome of the rear baldachin, lined with plant and flower ornament with a sun in the centre.

Agra Fort of the 1630s. The front baldachin, called *chatr* (honorific umbrella), under which originally stood the golden throne of Shah Jahan from where he overlooked the courtyard, stands out from the more sober architecture of the surrounding arcaded ranges. The rear baldachin provides the link to the arcades. The domes of both baldachins are supported by baluster-shaped columns, called cypress-bodied by Shah Jahan's historian Waris. The rich acanthus décor of their capitals announces bloom and flourishing, as does the adapted ancient Indian motif of the vase of plenty, *purna kalaśa*, which serves as their base. What has not been previously discussed is the ornamental lining of the domes, that gives us the key to the programme of the ensemble. The outer dome is covered with a trellis pattern diminishing in size towards the circle of the apex, in which appears a radiating sun (Fig. 1). The rear dome is lined with two concentric rings, filled by rich and dynamic flower and plant ornament (only partly preserved), in the apex of which is another sun (Fig. 2). The trellis pattern of the outer dome evokes a *jali* generated by the sun in the centre and brings to mind the poetic metaphor of the historian Muhammad Salih Kambo where he referred to the golden railing around the emperor's throne-baldachin (*jharokha*) in the palace of the Delhi Fort: for him it looked as if 'the rays of the sun were wound together'.[12]

The iconography of the baldachins was thus meant to convey the central thought of the ruling philosophy of Shah Jahan: as the king of the planets, the sun, brings nature to bloom, so the emperor makes the world flourish through his cosmic power, and, in a transferred sense, through his just and good government. He stands for the power of the sun and the spring, the renewal, generated in the real and ideal world. ◊

NOTES

1. Necipoğlu, "Early Modern Floral," 132–55.

2. Koch, "Jahangir as Francis Bacon's Ideal," 293–338; Koch, *The Complete Taj Mahal*, 2006 and 2012.

3. Skelton, "A Decorative Motif in Mughal Art," 147–52. After Skelton, Vivian A. Rich carried out a study of the influence of European herbals on Mughal floral representation in her unpublished dissertation for the School of Oriental and African Studies, London: V. A. Rich, "The Origins of Mughal Painting and its Development with particular Reference to the 17th and 18th Centuries", 1981; *eadem*, "Mughal Floral Painting and its European Sources," 183–89.

4. Jahangir's and Shah Jahan's painters knew and used illustrations of the scientific plant books of the later 16th century, such as those of Clusius, Lobelius, Dodoneus and Adrian Collaert, as well as the French florilegium of Pierre Valet, *Le Jardin du Roi très Chretien Henri IV*, Paris, 1608: see Koch, "Jahangir as Francis Bacon's Ideal" (cit. at n. 2).

5. Kalim, *Padshahnama*, f. 164a margin.

6. A brief overview of the development of *jali*s in India is given by Abbas, "Ornamental *Jali*s of the Mughals and their Precursors," 135–47.

7. Koch, *Complete Taj Mahal* (cit. at n. 2), 158–59, 164–65, 218–22.

8. *Mahjar* means screen, *musamman*, octagonal and *mushabbak*, latticed, trellised. These are the terms used by 'Abd al-Hamid Lahauri for the screen in his detailed description of the Taj Mahal, *Badshahnama*, ed. M. Kabir al-Din Aḥmad and M. 'Abd al-Rahim, Calcutta: Asiatic Society of Bengal, 1866–72, vol. 2, 324–25; translated in Koch, *Complete Taj Mahal* (cit. at n. 2), 256–57.

9. Koch, *Complete Taj Mahal* (cit. at n. 2), 215 and *passim*.

10. Kambo, *'Amal-i Salih/Shah Jahannama*, 187.

11. For this and the following, see Koch, "The Baluster Column," 45, 251–62; Koch, "Mughal Palace Gardens from Babur to Shah Jahan," 143–165.

12. Kambo, *'Amal-i Salih* (cit. at n. 10), vol. 3, 33.

Heavenly Gardens
The Imperial Mughal Style

"... latticed windows of white marble which are really
very pleasing to the eye."

Padshahnama of Waris, c. 1648

Shah Jahan, regarded as the greatest builder among the Mughal emperors, ushered in an age of spectacular achievement in architecture. His imperial vision gave rise to the majestic Taj Mahal tomb complex as well as mosques, palaces, royal fort enclosures and hunting lodges. Practically every ornamental detail of a Shah Jahani building is marked by its outstanding quality, and a number of fine techniques, including semi-precious stone inlay (*parchin kari*), painting and gilding, and stone carving, reached their zenith in this era. Many of the buildings of the age are described in the royal history of the period, the *Padshahnama* by the courtier Muhammad Waris. Among the details he furnishes are glowing mentions of the marble lattice screens, appearing to reference the 'Scales of Justice' *jali* screen in the Red Fort, Delhi: "One of these [arches] is towards the female quarters (*mashku-i mu 'ala*) and the other is towards the northern diwan and faces the Shah Mahal. In its front is fixed a white marble lattice-window, which, each night, had to be seen to be admired. The water of the *Nahr-i Bihisht* passes from beneath."[1]

In the inspired buildings of Shah Jahan, the *jali* form took a leap towards a new lyricism, breaking away from the rigid lines and geometric designs of the previous age. The paradisiacal imagery that informs the larger conceptual frameworks of grand tombs and palaces is brought to bear on the *jali*s too, as seen in the floral trellises around the central tomb chamber of the Taj Mahal, installed in 1647.[2] Flowers and trellises simulated a fantasy of nature, and *jali*s were set into facades forming larger decorative panels. The Moti Masjid at Agra built in 1653 has *jali*s of the floral trellis type at the focal end of its arcades (see p. 142 & fig. 1), making skilful play on the luminescent marble from which they are carved. No longer related to celestial mathematics alone, their organic forms have evolved towards the naturalism and wonder of nature, a hallmark of Mughal art. This formula was to hold sway for many subsequent centuries.

FACING PAGE & FIG. 1 (FOLLOWING PAGES) Floral trellis screen and detail, Moti Masjid, Agra, Uttar Pradesh, c. 1650

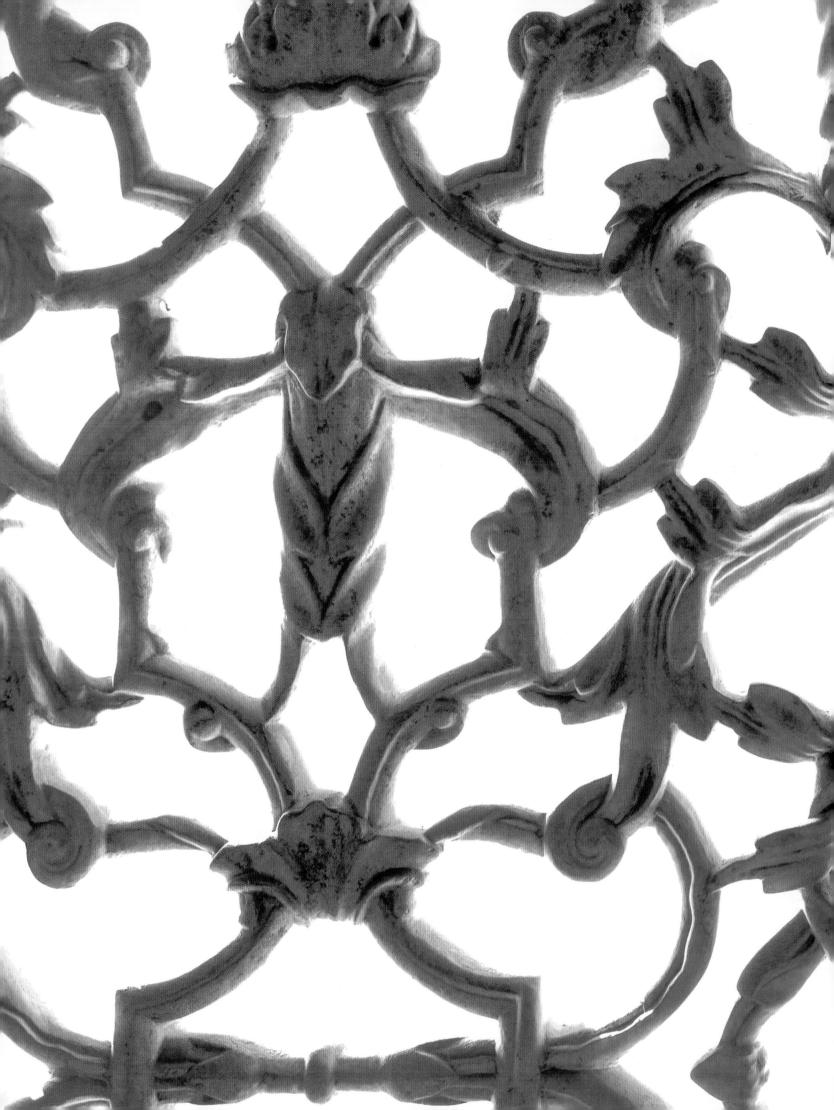

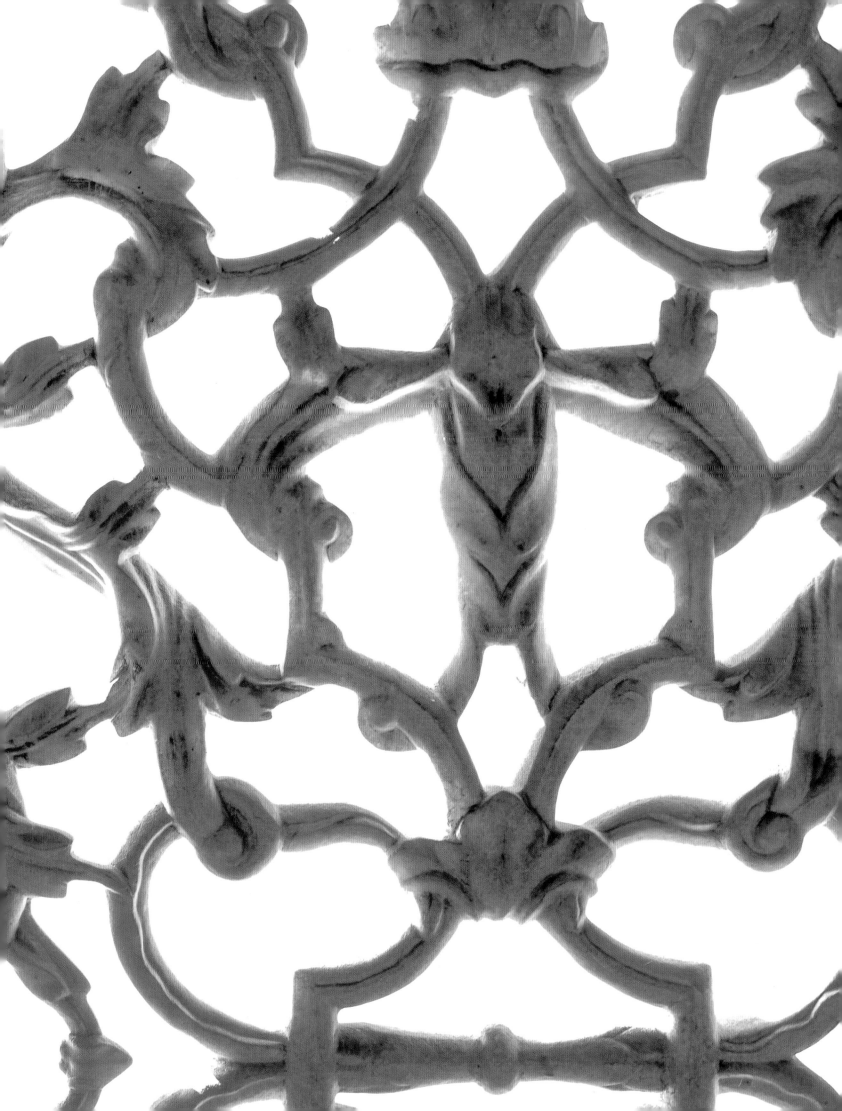

FIG. 2

FIG. 2
Detached floral trellis *jali* in the
style of the Taj Mahal screens,
c. 1645
Private collection, New York

❖ Floral Trellises

Floral trellises resemble undulating arabesque scrolls but with a broader spread and a geometric structure that underpins the naturalistic forms. The lines of the trellis are, in fact, stiffened organic vines, which hold blossoms, leaves and buds interwoven with cartouches. While arabesques tend to be reserved for borders around the field of carpets or edges of carved panels, a Mughal floral trellis grows into a tall rectangular panel that can form a low wall or a tall screen, enclosing a space in an organic embrace. Like geometric *jalis*, floral screens are often composed of multiple layered trellises within each other, which if separated would form logical and independent designs.

The inner chamber of the Taj Mahal represents an apex of the floral *jali* in the octagonal marble screen (*mahjar-i musamman-i mushabbak*) that surrounds the cenotaphs of Mumtaz Mahal and Shah Jahan (fig. 3). Beams of light entering the chamber from above cast dramatic shadows through this pierced enclosure. This marble lacework is, in fact, a replacement installed in 1643 in place of the original gold-enamelled screen made by the polymath goldsmith, lapidary and poet Sai'da Gilani (also known as Bibadal Khan) on the second death anniversary of Mumtaz in 1633.[3] The idea of such a screen surrounding cenotaphs perhaps loosely refers to the very simple burial style of the founder of Mughal empire, Babur, at Kabul.[4] The organic nature of the carving and the eight-fold nature of the screens evoke the paradisiacal imagery of heaven. The screens are topped with vase-shaped crenellations (*kanguras*) alternating with openwork volutes of acanthus leaves and smaller vases. Floral blossoms executed in *pietra dura* abound on and around the *jali*s. Of similar design, a closely related screen held now in a private collection (fig. 2) has a narrower and perhaps unfinished inlay border, but its main body is practically identical to the Taj screens.

In the 'Scales of Justice' *jali* at the Red Fort (fig. 4), so known because of the Europeanized motif of symbolic scales carved above, we see a combination of sensitively carved floral forms set within an ogival trellis interspersed with webbed cartouches. This variation of the floral trellis also employs ovoid cartouches placed at an angle in the corners of the central panel. Something of the spirit of this design is seen in a magnificent royal carpet woven at Lahore (fig. 5) in the same period. Artists, designers and craftsmen were drawn together in a splendid harmony of style, each echoing the imperial vision in their unique method.

Tall red sandstone trellises are to be found in the *burj* of the Agra Fort (fig. 6), framing the open view through filtered light. Their flattened treatment suggests that they are replacements for originals but, nevertheless, allow us to see the visual effect of the evening light streaming in through the floral trellises.

FOLLOWING PAGES
FIG. 3
Floral trellis *jali* wall (detail),
inner chamber, Taj Mahal, Agra,
Uttar Pradesh, c. 1643

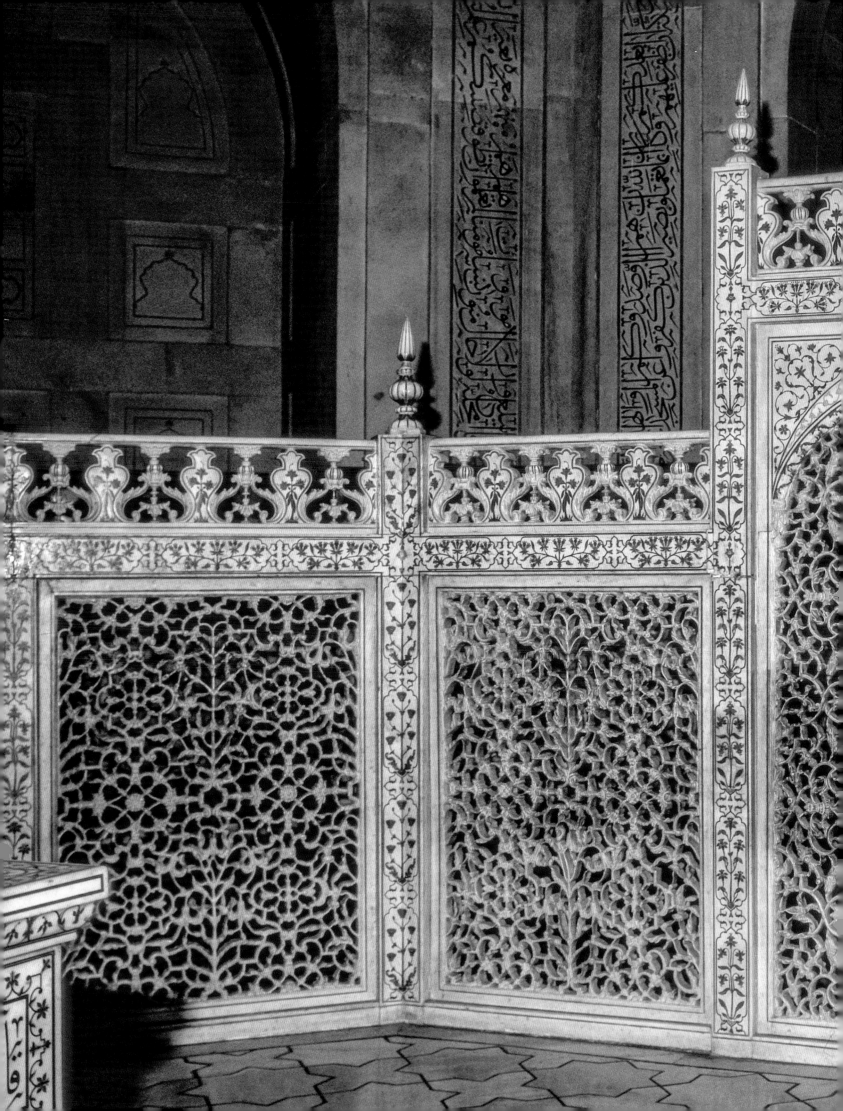

FIG. 5

FIG. 4
Damaged Scales of Justice *jali*,
Khas Mahal, 1639–48, Red Fort, Delhi,
photographed in 2019

FIG. 5
Fragment of a carpet with lattice and blossom
design, silk and pashmina wool, c. 1650,
The Metropolitan Museum of Art
Bequest of Benjamin Altman, 1913, 14.40.723

FOLLOWING PAGES
FIG. 6
Jali panels in *burj* pavilion, Khas Mahal,
Agra Fort, Uttar Pradesh, 1631–40

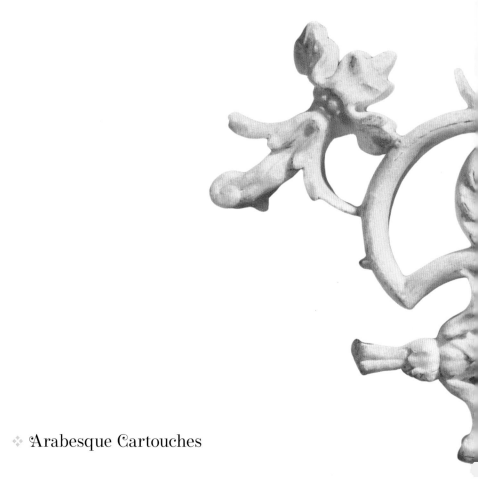

❖ Arabesque Cartouches

The term 'arabesque' is used to describe a characteristic feature of Islamicate vegetal ornament, consisting of rhythmic linear patterns of scrolling and interlacing foliage. Vines, split palmettes and abstract blossoms could be composed and arranged to fill spaces and cover surfaces, sometimes interwoven with ribbon-like cloud-bands of Chinese derivation. Illumination in painted folios was the natural home for delicate arabesques, where they decorated calligraphic texts and margins.

*Jali*s incorporated arabesque elements often in the spandrels of arches or in floral trellises. The *jali* medium was perfect for conveying the sense of ropey undulations and up-and-down twists and turns of the foliate forms and creating airy openings around cloud-bands. A fragment in a private collection (fig. 7) interweaves organic vines with smooth cartouches to create yet another variation on the idea of the arabesque.

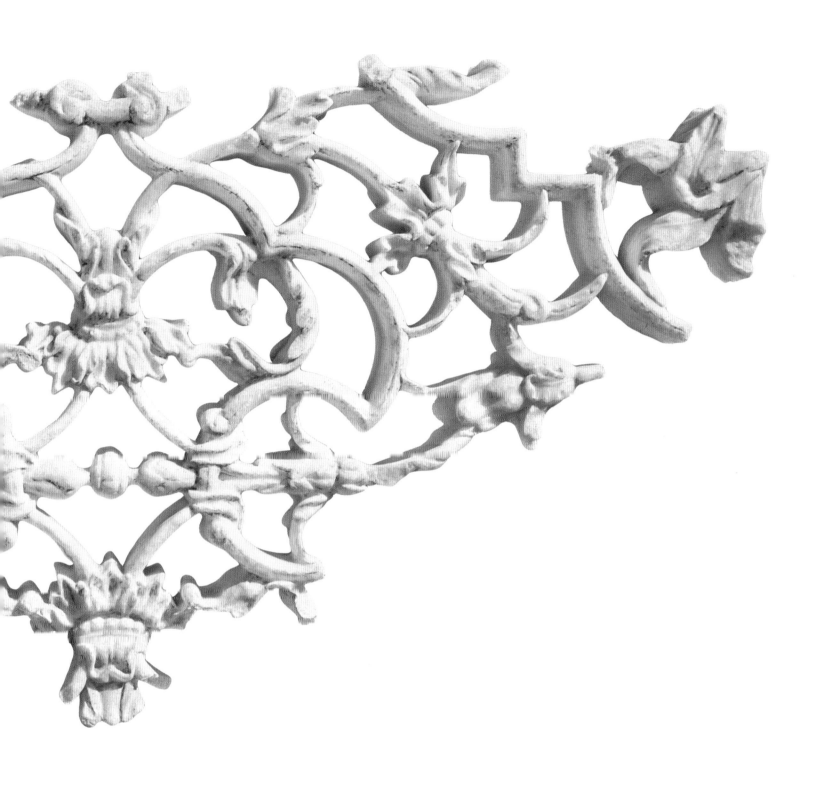

FIG. 7
Fragment of a *jali* with arabesques,
Mughal, mid-17th century,
Private collection, New Hampshire

FIG. 8

❖ Floral Vases

The motif of a vase or urn with rounded neck and high shoulders and spilling opulent flowers was an international one in the seventeenth century, shared between the decorative traditions of the Persianate, European and far Eastern courts. Chinese Meiping ceramic vases (so named for plum blossoms or plum wine) were shaped in this manner and depicted in Mughal painting as a type of imported ware.[5] In Dutch painting, the motif of a flowering vase is seen as a *vanitas* theme, associated with the transitory nature of earthly things, while in other contexts it played a more purely decorative role.[6] In the Indian tradition, the motif also evokes the ancient Hindu and Buddhist symbol of the auspicious Urn of Plenty (*purna kalasha*), although in artistic renderings the urn typically tends to be small.

In Mughal architectural ornament, floral vases evolved from formal and slightly stiff motifs in the inlaid and painted decoration of the late Jahangir period into a more opulent feature in Shah Jahan's buildings. Furthermore, craftsmen were tasked with newly realizing the motif in the form of a *jali*. The long, rectangular inner hall of

FIG. 8
Facade with five floral vase
*jali*s, Diwan-i Khas, Agra Fort,
Uttar Pradesh, 1631

the Diwan-i Khas in the Agra Fort contains two facing friezes of five identical openwork vases placed above large arched openings. The far wall is dressed richly with shallow niches and holds a long inlaid inscription above the series of refined and almost identical floral vase *jali*s (fig. 8). The inscription names God, the Prophet Muhammad and the first four Caliphs in roundels interspersed between verses from the Persian poet Kashani and the date of the building (1631).[7] Each *jali* consists of a tall-necked urn made up of floral scrolls and holding flowering sprays, which flow symmetrically across the space, carved almost in the round (fig. 9). Their abundance and elevated position echoes the spirit of praise and celebration of the poem.

Floral vase *jali*s began to appear in buildings in Rajasthan and the Deccan, such as the Sheesh Mahal at the Amer Fort and the Bibi ka Maqbara tomb complex in Aurangabad. While the motif varied stylistically, such flowering vase *jali*s generally followed the Shah Jahani formula of being placed at a height.

FOLLOWING PAGES
FIG. 9
Floral vase *jali* (detail), Diwan-i Khas, Agra Fort, c. 1631

❖ Italianate Motifs

In addition to flowering urns, other Europeanizing motifs such as lyres, interlocking baroque foliates and lobed cartouches made their way into Mughal architectural decoration by the middle of the seventeenth century. The presence of Florentine craftsmen at the Mughal court involved in the development of *pietra dura* likely introduced some of these motifs (fig. 10). In the world of *jali*s, comparable designs appear in various guises, some familiar and others unique to this element of architecture. Curving acanthus leaves and short balusters form oval-shaped openings in a low *jali* wall (fig. 11) located in the Taj Mahal's mosque building. A typical Venetian knot motif can be seen in the interlocked trellis of the Moti Mahal (see p. 142). The bold and spiky cartouche-and-spear design of a small marble railing in the Nagina Masjid (fig. 12) in the Agra Fort incorporates lyres and volutes as well, with the spears rising up as three-dimensional leafy points. A sandstone railing with lyre and volute shapes (fig. 13) appears in another part of the fort.

FIG. 10
Details from a folio from an instructional book of ornamental designs by Nicolas Guérard, *Livre Nouveau de Prinsipes D'Ornemens...*, *Plate 4*, c. 1715–1725
The Metropolitan Museum of Art, The Elisha Whittlesey Collection, The Elisha Whittlesey Fund, 1949
Accession number 49.69.17(4)

FACING PAGE
FIG. 11
Jali railing with oval cartouches, mosque, Taj Mahal complex, completed 1653

FOLLOWING PAGES
FIG. 12
Small railing with interlocking lyres, cartouches and floral spears (detail), Nagina Masjid, Agra Fort, Uttar Pradesh, 1631–40

FIG. 13
Detail of *jali* railing with lyres and volutes, Agra Fort, c. 1637

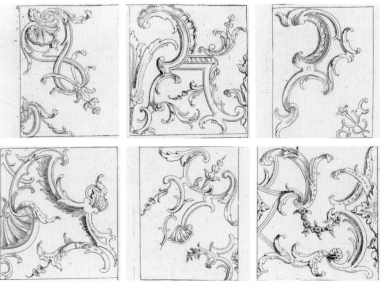

FIG. 10

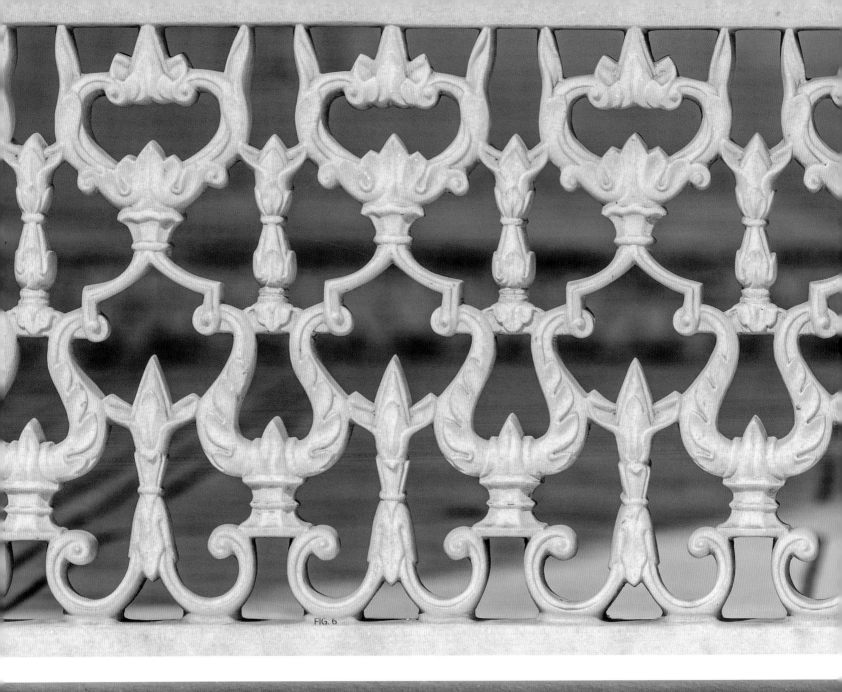

FIG. 6

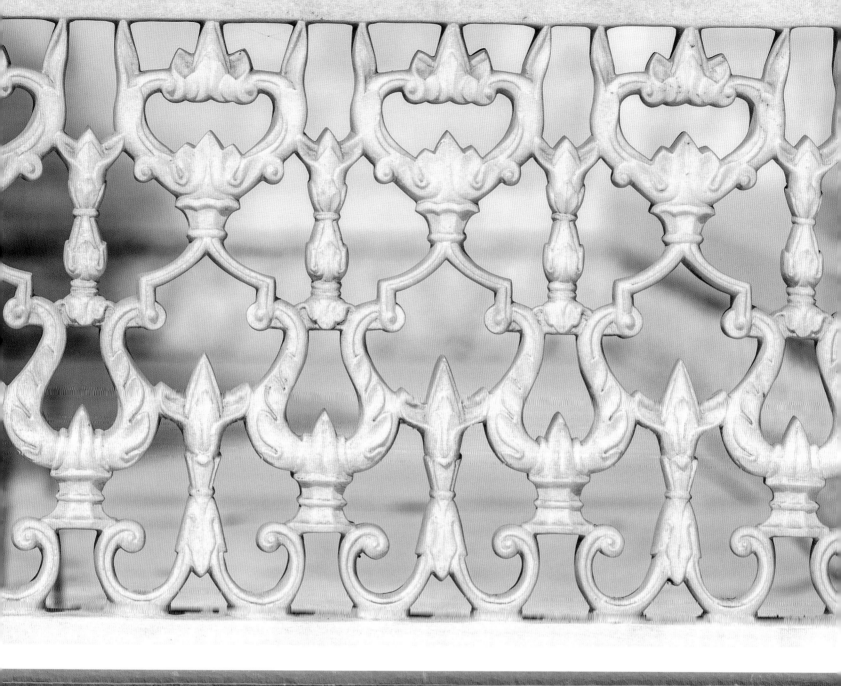

FIG. 14

✦ Naturalistic Flowers and Plants

Naturalistically rendered flowers and leaves evolved in early seventeenth-century Mughal art (fig. 14) from botanical studies wherein flowering plants were accurately depicted from root to blossom with close attention to every detail. The painters Mansur and Abu'l Hasan are especially renowned for their sensitive observations. Jahangir's famed love of nature had laid the foundation for this artistic focus in painting, and under his patronage individual floral forms came to be carved in stone relief too. These are found on the front and back ends of the cenotaph of Akbar at Sikandra (1614) where individual plant studies fill the field around the inscriptions (see pp. 116–117). Later, by about 1640, the Mughal decorative arts had widely adopted the repeating motif of a single formal flower, often under a cusped arch, which appeared in tent panels, hangings, carvings, and also the most ambitious *jali*s.

The Shah Burj, built between 1631 and 1640 by Shah Jahan, is a spectacular part of the Agra Fort with an ornately decorated fountain room. The central arch of the room is surmounted by a lunette *jali* containing naturalistically rendered irises and other flowering plants and bushes (fig. 15). Such *jali*s also adorned the lunettes on the river-face of the same palace room. Their elite locations indicate the high place accorded to such naturalistic *jali*s, which complement the sensitive natural relief carvings in the walls all around. The Lahore Fort boasts grand *jali*s in its Sheesh Mahal

FIG. 14
Yellow Narcissus and Butterfly,
signed Muhammad Nadir of
Samarkand, 205 x 110 mm,
c. 1620, Private collection, Mumbai

of striking cartouche arch shapes inscribed onto a marble webbing (fig. 16). A central *jharokha* window opening is surrounded by a frame of prunuses, irises and other flowering plants, and includes a subtle flowering vase among the foliage above.

The site of the mosque and tomb complex of Ghaziuddin in Delhi contains examples of some of the most impressive floral *jalis* of the late seventeenth century. Built by a high ranking officer in the service of Aurangzeb. The mosque building has a pair of monumental archways on each side, both containing tall *jalis* carved from red sandstone (fig. 17). The screens are divided into sections, each containing a naturalistically carved flowering plant, such as iris, lily and tulip (fig. 18). In the mosque courtyard are finely carved screens and doors (figs 19, 20) with elegantly carved single flowers. At the Moti Masjid in Delhi built by Aurangzeb in 1663, an expressively carved vine with leaves forms the arch below the *minbar* (fig. 21). Although this feature is not a *jali* per se, it shares the carving and sculptural techniques.

The influential floral *jali* grew in popularity for the next few centuries, but the elegance, restraint and monumentality of the seventeenth-century examples was not often matched. Already in the carving at Ghaziuddin's mosque a certain stiffness in the carving may be discerned, although the grandeur and scale of the *jalis* make up for this tendency.

FOLLOWING PAGES
FIG. 15
Lunette *jali* with irises and other flowering plants, Shah Burj, Agra Fort, Uttar Pradesh, c. 1630–35

FIG. 16
Jali in Sheesh Mahal, Lahore Fort, Pakistan, c. 1634

FIG. 15

FIG. 16

FIGs 17 (FACING PAGE) & 18
Jali screen with flowers in
each section and details,
Tomb complex of Ghaziuddin,
Delhi, late 17th century

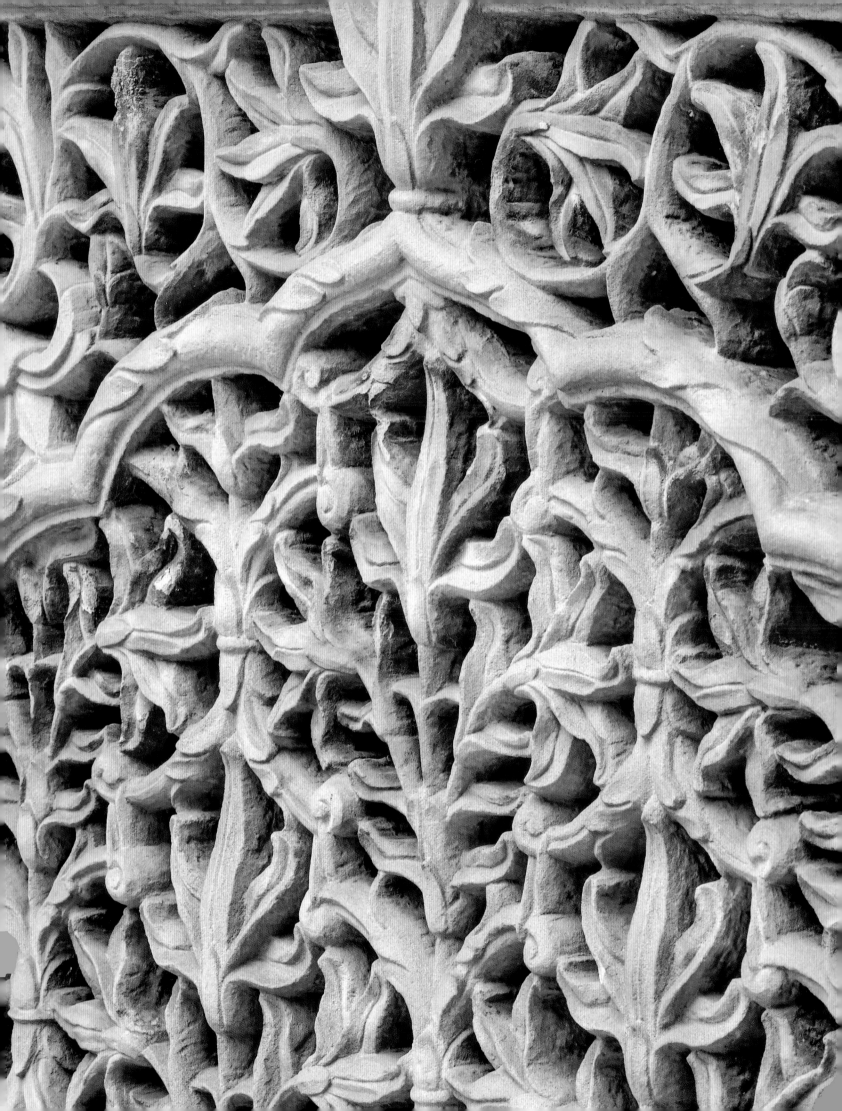

FIG. 20

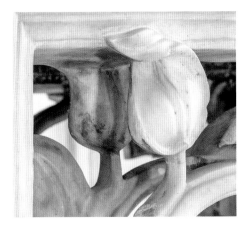

FIG. 21

FIG. 19 (FACING PAGE) & FIG. 20
Jali screens at the tomb complex of
Ghaziuddin, Delhi, late 17th century

FIG. 21
Minbar steps, detail of carved leaf,
Moti Masjid, Red Fort, Delhi, c. 1660

❖ Chini Khana

One of the most distinctive and delightful Mughal architectural features to have emerged in the period of Jahangir is that of the small, recessed niche, known as a *chini khana* ('china-house' or niche for holding ceramic vessels, but also, at times, an oil lamp). This niche appears in various shapes, usually as a plain or cusped arch but also in the form of a cutout flower-head or lobed cartouche. Wall niches become ubiquitous in Mughal architecture by the middle of the seventeenth century, appearing in deep carving, shallow relief, inlay and occasionally in completely cutout style.

A *chini khana* straddles the symbolic worlds of spiritual and royal association. On one hand, the image of a small arch with a hanging lamp (*mishkah*), or source of illumination, evokes the famous Light Verse in the Qur'an, which has provided inspiration for the leitmotif in Islamic art and for the designs of prayer *mihrab*s in architecture from Gujarat to Bengal. On the other, the niche is used to house worldly objects and decorative motifs (fig. 22) such as bottles and floral vases. One ambitious version of the *chini khana* design places bands of repeating niches behind a waterfall (*aabshar*) such as in the Shalimar Bagh in Srinagar and the Diwan-i Khas in the Agra Fort.[8] The niches could hold lamps at night and flowers in the day whose illumination and colour could be seen through the carved cascading water. The motif goes on beyond the courtly realm, into everyday life where the simple mud hut in rural India is adorned with the timeless feature of a *chiragh khana*, niche in a wall to place an oil lamp.

The walls of *baradari* pavilions built along the edge of the Ana Sagar lake in Ajmer are decorated with *chini khana* niches (fig. 23) and executed in a way that takes wondrous advantage of the sunlight. These marble walls are cut to a thinness that allows light to come through the back of the niche, creating an illuminated effect at the times of day when the light is strong.

FIG. 22

FIG. 22
Chini khana panel installed with works of art, displaying Japanese metalwork.
Private collection, New Hampshire

FOLLOWING PAGES
FIG. 23
Baradari with *chini khana* decoration, Ana Sagar, Ajmer, Rajasthan, 1637

FIG. 24

The *chini khana* style in Iran is most notably seen at the shrine at Ardebil, which underwent major renovations under Shah Abbas I, and in the cut plaster *muqarna*s in the music room (fig. 24) of the Ali Qapu pavilion at Isfahan (completed 1653). The decoration of the music room in Isfahan takes on the shapes of bottles and vessels, among other cutouts. Parallels in northern India can be seen in the eighteenth-century tombs at Nuh (fig. 25) and in the *ghat* wall complex attributed to Raja Bharmal at Vrindavan, where profiles of bending bottles are cut out of stone walls (fig. 26), allowing the light to enter the darkened chamber through these lyrical shapes.

FIG. 25

FIG. 27
Jali with hexagonal pattern,
Agra Fort, Uttar Pradesh,
mid-17th century

FOLLOWING PAGES
FIG. 28
Wall with geometric *jali*s, Agra Fort,
mid-17th century

FIG. 29
Cusped *jali*s with hexagonal
design, Taj Mahal, Agra, 1653

*Jali*s with geometric hexagons, stars and polygons are found largely in outer walls and border screens in the royal commissions of Shah Jahan. These designs are often reserved for less prestigious locations and serve a practical rather than decorative function. One such screen, detached from its site and now in the Metropolitan Museum of Art, has a strong double trellis pattern of outer hexagons and inner octagons, interspaced with smaller pierced diamonds (see p. 8). It is reputed to have once been in a pavilion of the Ana Sagar lake in Ajmer. A large hexagonal *jali* wall located in the Agra Fort encloses star medallions forming a fine web between areas of the court (fig. 27). Not far from this installation, bold and broad hexagonal screens alternate with pairs of star screens, lining up to form the outer wall of the courtyard, surmounted by crenellations (fig. 28). The lower level of the Taj Mahal also makes use of geometric *jali*s (fig. 29), demonstrating the hierarchical position of these types of screens.

FIG. 27

❖ Facades

An exceptional facade that combines the *chini khana* style with geometric-style *jali*s can be seen on the outer wall of the so-called *chhatri* of Jaswant Singh in Agra (completed 1658). Built by Raja Jaswant Singh, in honour of his slain elder brother Amar Singh Rathore of Marwar, the central structure is a twelve-pillared red sandstone mesh building resting in a rectangular courtyard. The outer wall is decorated with diamond-shaped cutouts in arched screens (fig. 30), set in walls decorated with bottles in the shape of rosewater sprinklers (*gulabpash*) in cusped arches (fig. 31).

The Lal Mahal hunting lodge built by Shah Jahan at Rupbas, Rajasthan, in 1637 presents an evocative facade of octagonal *jali* kiosks set on water (fig. 32), with delightful ornamental details. Taking its name from the red sandstone, the palace comprises several small buildings with walled enclosures, some overlooking the lake set on a raised walkway. ⊗

FIG. 30
Jali at the *chhatri* of Raja Jaswant Singh, Agra, Uttar Pradesh, 1658

FOLLOWING PAGES
FIG. 31
*Jali*s surrounded by *gulabpash*es in cusped arches, *chhatri* of Raja Jaswant Singh, Agra, 1658

FIG. 30

FIG. 32
Lal Mahal hunting lodge,
ornamental detail, Rupbas,
Rajasthan, 17th century

NOTES

1. Rezavi, "The Mighty Defensive Fort," 1116.

2. Koch, *The Complete Taj Mahal*, 256–57.

3. Ibid., 167–70.

4. Ibid., 167.

5. A depiction from the *Jahangirnama* of the courtly ceremony of the weighing of Prince Khurram includes Chinese ceramics, including a Meiping type vase, in the background (British Museum 1948,1009,0.69).

6. Koch, *Complete Taj Mahal*, 219.

7. According to the late Abdullah Ghouchani: The inscription comes from the *diwan* of Abu Talib–i Kalim–i Kashani (Kashani 1957 [1336], *Diwan*, 339–340). The inscription on the building however shows verses that are not included in the *divan* and which are in a different order. The date of the building according to the poem is mentioned in the last line in *abjad* letters—1040 AH (1631 AD)—*sa'adat saray humayun asas* [the happiness of the court of Humayun is the foundation]. *An dil gusha qasr ali bana Sar-i Akbarabad shud arsh sa / Buvad kungaresh az jabin-i sipar Namayan chu dandan-i sin-i sipihr / Sujud dar in saray-i surur Kunad sar-nivisht bad az jabhe dur / Sharafat yeki aye dar shan-i u Sa'adat dar aghush-i ivan-i u / Rah-i jur ar bishukam basteh ast Be zanjir-i 'adlesh setam basteh ast / Be nazam be zanjir kaz 'adl-i shah Hame chashm shud dar rahe dad-khah / Bar akhwan-i mardum chinan sar-i hisab Ke danad che bebeenad shabha be khwab / Dar ivan-i shahi be-sad ihtisham Chu khurshid bar charkh bada mudam / Chu ivan-u 'alam arai shud Sar-i khak az u asman sai shud / Shahansha-i afaq shah Jahan Ke nazad be u ruh-i sahib qiran / Be-in raunaq wa zib va zinat makan Nadeede bar ruye zamin asman / Buvad sahn- bamesh chu seema-i mihr Be-ziresh futahdeh chu saye-yi sipihr / Be-tarikhesh andishe avard ru Dar-i fez shud baz az chahar su / Chunin guft taba'a haqayiq shinas (sa'adat saray va humayun asas).* In the florets from the middle: *Allah Muhhamad / Abu bakr* (on the right) / *'Umar* (left) / *'Usman* (on the right of Abu Bakr) / *'Ali* (on the left of 'Umar).

8. Moynihan, *Paradise as a Garden*, 138.

Fantasy and Formality
The Deccan *Jali*

*"I am searching for my beloved who has hidden herself
behind the thin curtain of eyelashes."*

Sultan Ibrahim 'Adil Shah II, 17th century

The Deccan sultanates, which flourished alongside the Mughal world, developed distinctive styles of art and architecture, often characterized as fantastical and visually opulent while also staying classically formal. The unique character of Deccan art was partly shaped by its connections to the outer world. The region was linked to Iran and the Middle East through dynastic lineages, Shi'a Islam and spiritual and courtly figures who traversed those worlds. A growing European presence in the coastal regions brought further artistic and cultural influences to the aesthetics that flourished in the Deccan.

Like much of the region's art and architecture, the *jali*s of the Deccan display a variety of forms. Two *jali*s exemplify contrasting styles associated with Bijapur, one of the five sultanates that flourished in the sixteenth and seventeenth centuries. One of these two is an example carved in sandstone found in the finely finished tomb of 'Adil Shahi governor Sidi 'Abdul Malik 'Aziz at Badami, in Karnataka. The *jali* window arch (fig. 1) contains circular and floral medallions surmounted by a pair of rampant felines flanking a lotus bud finial. The close proximity of the site to the ancient Badami caves is recalled in these sculptural elements. A contrasting arabesque style is seen in an iron *jali* lodged now in the All Saints Church at Bijapur (fig. 2). It has been attributed to the late sixteenth or early seventeenth century and admired for its Persianate ornamental foliates.[1] The screen was found in excavations at the site of the so-called Chini Mahal at Bijapur and was perhaps part of a Persianate structure that housed imported Chinese ceramics.

FACING PAGE
Zigzag diagonal pattern of polygons at Maqbara Shams al-Umara, Paigah tomb complex, Hyderabad, Telangana, late 19th–20th century

FIG. 1

Jali with rampant lions from the tomb
of Sidi 'Abdul Malik 'Aziz, Badami,
Karnataka, late 16th–early 17th century

FACING PAGE
FIG. 2

Iron *jali* with arabesques, set in a wooden
frame, All Saints Church, Bijapur,
Karnataka, late 16th–early 17th century

FIG. 3
One of the two surviving
calligraphic *jali*s with Qur'anic
verses (detail), Tomb of Ibrahim
'Adil Shah, Bijapur, Karnataka, 1626

FIG. 5

FIG. 6

FIG. 7

FACING PAGE
FIG. 4
Calligraphic *jali* with Qur'anic
verses set in an arch, Tomb
of Ibrahim 'Adil Shah, Bijapur,
Karnataka, 1626

FIG. 5
Calligraphic *jali* at a tomb complex,
undated, Yarkand, China

FIG. 6
Pierced wall detail, tomb of 'Isa
Khan Tarkhan II, Makli, Pakistan,
mid-17th century

FIG. 7
Screen fragment with letters
against a pierced scroll,
Nishapur, Iran, 12th century
The Metropolitan Museum of Art,
Rogers Fund, 1940, 40.170.444

Perhaps, the most accomplished style to be found at Bijapur is that of calligraphic *jalis* found at the Ibrahim Rauza, the seventeenth-century garden tomb of Sultan Ibrahim 'Adil Shah (figs 3, 4). These openwork *jalis* are the last two surviving of several such carved screens that were set in the upper arches surrounding the inner sepulchre. The most complete *jali* allows us to discern the scope of the original scheme. Qur'anic verses in interlace calligraphy fill the lunette.[2] The powerful letters rest on slimmer supports of scrolling ornament, and, remarkably, a small section of the *jali* may be read in reverse from the inside of the building. This calligraphic style in a *jali* mode is rare, however, a related example in wood appears in a tomb complex at Yarkand, in Xinjiang, China (fig. 5).[3] At the necropolis in Makli, Sindh (now Pakistan), a geometric piercing in the sepulchral chamber (fig. 6) of 'Isa Khan Tarkhan II (d. 1651–52) may serve as a simplified form of pierced pseudo-calligraphy (i.e., a calligraphic-like inscription, carving or feature but only decorative in nature). From a much earlier period, a fragment of a ceramic glazed screen with carved letters on an epigraphic band against a vegetal scroll was excavated in Nishapur, Iran (fig. 7), indicating that the origins of the style might lie in the medieval period.

Related calligraphic effects are seen in the metalwork *'alams* or standards of Shi'a centres in the Deccan. One striking example is fashioned in the shape

FIG. 8

FIG. 9

FIG. 10

FIG. 8
Gilt-copper processional *'alam*
(standard) with pierced calligraphy,
fabricated as a falcon, Deccan,
17th century
Victoria and Albert Museum,
IM 163-1913

FIG. 9
Pierced-bronze candlestick
inscribed with good wishes, Iran,
c. 1500
The Metropolitan Museum of Art,
Purchase, The Seley Foundation
Inc. Gift, Louis E. and Theresa S.
Seley Purchase Fund for Islamic
Art, Schimmel Foundation Inc.,
Margaret Mushekian and Mr. and
Mrs. Jerome A. Straka Gifts, Rogers
and The Friends of the Islamic
Department Funds, 1980, 1980.114

FIG. 10
Cut-steel calligraphic plaque, Iran,
c. late 17th century
The Metropolitan Museum of Art,
Rogers Fund, 1987, 1987.14

of a falcon, its body made up of letters of a Shi'a call to prayer, the Nadi 'Ali
(fig. 8). The taste for interlace calligraphy was also favoured in Timurid Iran as
in its decorative arts and in architectural ornament. A candleholder attributed
to Khurasan in the late fifteenth century displays a pierced *Thuluth* inscription
on the main body, with benedictory wishes for its owner (fig. 9). This design
cleverly applies the idea of light and silhouette in a functional object that itself
is the bearer of light. Another instance of the use of openwork calligraphy is in
a cartouche-shaped plaque, created from a single sheet of solid steel, whose
wide, flat border encloses a hemistich referring to Fatima and her sons (fig. 10).
Such plaques, which served both a decorative and invocative function, were often

FIG. 11

FIG. 12

set in the doors of shrines, mosques, and theological schools. While the decorative arts of Persia and India displayed the use of pierced calligraphy in this manner, the style did not generally move to buildings, therefore the *jalis* at the Ibrahim Rauza are quite exceptional.

Deccani sultanate architecture favoured stucco decoration and some of the most impressive *jalis*, including very large ones, are made from delicate stucco. Among the Qutb Shahi tombs of the rulers of Golconda, the Begum Hayat Bakhsh mosque built in the late seventeenth century contains discrete and charming stucco *jalis* placed high above the doorways. Among them is a distinctive design with large chrysanthemum-style blossoms set on a diagonal grid within a pointed arch (fig. 11).

Deccani *jalis* were also influenced by the imperial Mughal style, as were many of the other courtly arts. The Bibi ka Maqbara tomb in Aurangabad, built in 1660–61 for the wife of the Mughal emperor Aurangzeb, is often referred to as a smaller version of the Taj Mahal at Agra but adds a sumptuous Deccani flourish to the decorative features (fig. 12). At this monument, vase *jalis* are florid and opulent while tall

FIG. 11
Juli window with large blossoms, Begum Hayat Mosque, Qutb Shahi tomb complex, Hyderabad, Telangana, completed 1672

FIG. 12
An openwork carved *jali* vase, Bibi ka Maqbara, Aurangabad, Maharashtra, 1660–61

screens around the entrances display a repeating pattern of delicate webbing held within ogival trellises (fig. 13). The grave markers of the interred figures rest at a lower level. As at the Taj Mahal, the entire zone is surrounded by an octagonal *jali* screen, leaving the graves open above and to be viewed from an upper balcony. This design came to be the preferred style for royal tombs, from Aurangzeb's to Muhammad Shah's, where low walls of simple repeating *jali* form and open skies were the norm. This *jaal* effect also became popular in the development of textiles, which could easily reproduce the same rhythmic pattern on a loom.

Perhaps the most vivid *jali*s of the Deccan are to be found in its final phase of traditional architecture, in the tombs of the Paigah family—important courtiers of the Nizams of Hyderabad. This evocative site of the late eighteenth to early twentieth century contains a necropolis complex of graves (fig. 14) with an adjoining mosque. The buildings are composed of marble elements and elaborately decorated with mainly lime and stucco carved ornament. The cosmopolitan styles and myriad motifs have evoked parallels with 'Moorish', Rajput, Mughal and east Asian decoration and include several exceptional stucco lattices, relief-carved panels and *jali* doors (figs 15–20, also see p. 188). Among them is a screen with star-and-hexagon design and carved to refined slimness, one with a zigzag diagonal pattern of polygons and a closed *jali* with deeply cut fan-like designs. Set among other imaginative decorative features such as pineapple-shaped finials on chevron carved stems, twisted dome toppers and floriated arabesques, the inventive *jali*s harmonize with kindred fantastical elements of late Deccan architecture.

FIG. 14

FACING PAGE
FIG. 13
Jali work and floral carvings
on facade of Bibi ka Maqbara,
Aurangabad, Maharashtra, 1661

FIG. 14
Maqbara Shams al-Umara,
Paigah tomb complex, Hyderabad,
Telangana, late 18th to early
20th century

PAGES 200–202
FIGs 15–20
Stucco lattices, relief-carved panels
and *jali* doors at Maqbara Shams
al-Umara, Paigah tomb complex

FIG. 20

FIG. 21

FIG. 21
European-style *jali* earrings,
c. 1930s
Private collection, Philadelphia

These expressive patterns continue to inspire modern life of the Deccan in vivid forms. A pair of Georgian-style earrings in a private collection take the form of curving roundels enclosed in a flower-and-bow diamond frame encircling a stiffened *jali* mesh of single diamonds set at cross points between intersecting wires (fig. 21). The earrings were once part of an unknown 1930s ornament, but later reworked by a Bombay art dealer in the 1990s, describing them as Hyderabadi *jali* earrings.[4]

The traditional cashew and sugar biscuits of Hyderabad, known locally as *badam ki jali* and bought to celebrate special occasions, are stamped with geometric cutout shapes reminiscent of the many *jali*s found in the Qutb Shahi and Nizami architecture of this historic city in the centre of the Deccan. ⊗

NOTES

1. Welch, *India: Art and Culture*, 289, fig. 192; Cousens, *Bijapur*, 66, fig. 15.

2. Ghouchani, *Inscriptions on Nishabur Pottery*, 1986.

3. Thanks are due to George Michell for sharing this information.

4. Records kindly provided by the owner.

Jali Mania
From Rajputs to the Raj

"I know the planets talk at night and tell secrets
about You."

Mirabai, 16th century

Once established, the formal Mughal *jali*, like so many other idioms of art and architecture, evolved into a delightful variety of themes and styles over the course of the eighteenth to twentieth centuries. The *jali* form was expanded and diversified, made of a range of materials and put to many decorative and functional uses. These are most clearly seen in the architecture of Rajasthan and central India, in palaces of the maharajas, and even in early twentieth-century Indo-British buildings such as Edwin Lutyens's design for the Viceroy's House—now the Rashtrapati Bhavan in New Delhi.

In the courtly setting, *jali*s served to screen off the *zenana* (women's quarter) from public gaze and were employed in almost all the forts and palaces of princely Rajasthan. While they had the desired effect of segregating the sexes, in the artistic imagination *jali* screens also sparked a sense of mystery and allure for what lay beyond. Life behind the *jali* screen became a point of fascination partly because it was the most powerful and inaccessible women who were concealed from gaze. A painting from the *Mandi Bhagavata* reveals the social order of women at court, where those of less exalted status are prominent while the elite are glimpsed through pierced screens (fig. 1).[1] Raja Kansa is shown at centre, listening to the prophecy communicated by an old duenna while other women attend on him and provide courtly entertainment.

FIG. 1

FIG. 1
Raja Kansa listens to the prophecy of an old duenna, folio (detail) from *Bhagavata Purana* series, Mandi, c. 1635–50
Private collection, Mumbai

FIG. 2
Amer Fort, Rajasthan, late 17th century

Flanking this scene are tall red *jali*s—possibly indicating *pinajra-kari* (woodwork) of the Kashmir region—shielding the secluded world of his wives, but offering a glimpse through a little window opening.[2] The manner of creating a cutout window in the middle of a *jali* screen appears in many architectural compositions, including in a large geometric and floral *jali* wall at Amber Fort (fig. 2).

*Jali*s allowed women to be part of wider courtly spectacles and events, particularly as some balcony screens were carved at a downward angle that would provide arena or street views. A painting of c. 1730–40 attributed to the painter Nainsukh depicts the Mughal emperor Muhammad Shah witnessing an elephant fight from a *jharokha* window (fig. 3). The ladies of the court also view the event, although from behind hatched screens that flank the emperor.

The literary imagination too was fired by the metaphorical possibilities of the *jali*. Among them is the conceit of a building dressed as a veiled woman.[3] *Jali*s, with their interlace patterns that resemble woven textiles, can be seen to act as a veil

FIG. 2

for women in the *zenana* quarters. Behind the *jali*, women were active writers of Persian *masnavi*s, Urdu *ghazal*s, Braj Bhasha poetry and other forms of literature. For example, at the court of Kishangarh, Bani Thani or Vishnupriya, beloved of the poet-prince Savant Singh, was an author in her own right. In a Kishangarh painting of the mid-eighteenth century, she appears in shadowy form behind a screen in a pavilion while the prince gazes up at her from a garden terrace below (fig. 4).

The desert forts and palaces of Rajasthan are famed for their *jali* work, where lengthy facades are covered with intricately carved screens that are integrated alongside dense carving and other forms of ornament. Typical of the Rajput style was the combination of a deeply curving *bangla*-eave style roof or cusped arches surmounting the *jali* screen. One of the most recognizable buildings of Rajasthan, the Hawa Mahal (Palace of the Winds) in Jaipur offers a spectacular facade featuring these elements (see p. 204). Shaped like the rising crown (*mukut*) of Krishna, the pierced facade allowed breezes to flow and offered its occupants views of the Pink City's street life while integrating coloured glass into the openings.

FIG. 3

FIG. 3
Muhammad Shah and a consort watching
an elephant fight from a *jali* enclosure
(detail), Attributed to Nainsukh, Guler
(Himachal Pradesh), c. 1730–40
Cleveland Museum of Art, John L.
Severance Fund, 2005.1.a

FIG. 4
Maharaja Kumar Sawant Singh of
Kishangarh gazing up at Bani Thani in a
screened pavilion (detail), c. 1745
Harvard Art Museums/Arthur M. Sackler
Museum, Gift in gratitude to John Coolidge,
Gift of Leslie Cheek, Jr., Anonymous
Fund in memory of Henry Berg, Louise
Haskell Daly, Alpheus Hyatt, Richard
Norton Memorial Funds and through the
generosity of Albert H. Gordon and Emily
Rauh Pulitzer; formerly in the collection of
Stuart Cary Welch, Jr., 1995.114

FIG. 4

FIG. 5

The Junagarh fort at Bikaner, dating to the sixteenth century with later additions, exhibits the lavish use of multi-tiered *jharokha* windows and *jali* screens in internal courtyards, such as in the seventeenth-century Karan Mahal or a later-time Anup Mahal or the Phool Mahal (fig. 5). A lyrical effect produced by the combination of wall paintings and coloured glass-fitted *jali*s is seen throughout in the interior

FIG. 5
Phool Mahal, Junagarh Fort
Bikaner, Rajasthan, c. 17th century

FIG. 6

corridors. Light filters in through the starry openings in various hues, setting off a delightful interplay with gesso-painted and gilded wall surfaces, techniques in the palace decoration that claim Florentine inspiration. Also at Bikaner, an old courtyard in the twentieth-century Lalgarh Palace (1902–26) boasts up to four levels of *jali*s, creating a monumental filigree facade.

Among the most striking of Rajasthani *jali* facades are those at the majestic fort of Mehrangarh at Jodhpur, built and expanded from the fifteenth to the eighteenth centuries by the Rathore rulers. Dramatic transitions of styles are seen in the Shringara Chowk (courtyard) where exuberant facades of screened *jharokha* windows from different phases of development intersect at fanciful angles (fig. 6).

FIG. 6
Shringara Chowk,
Mehrangarh Fort, Jodhpur,
Rajasthan, 15th to 17th century

FIG. 7

FIG. 8

Now detached from its original setting, possibly an early twentieth-century Jain temple or shrine, is a metalwork-and-wood *jali* screen door (fig. 7) with figural images in the upper part. Cut from sheet metal, the iconographic theme contains images of pilgrimage and worship, visitations to seated icons, and various attendant figures. The style suggests that the images are drawn from devotional paintings or cloth hangings—in some ways resembling the early-twentieth century 'net' *pichhvai*s produced in Europe for export to India—setting individual compositions against an openwork ground of trellis designs and leafy cutouts.[4]

Alluding to the solar and lunar lineages of the Rajput clans, pierced sun and moon motifs 'wink' in the wall of a chamber in a Jaisalmer *haveli* (fig. 8), creating a somewhat anthropomorphic effect.

FIG. 7
Screen with figural images in metal and wood, Gujarat or Rajasthan, early 20th century
Manglam Arts, Jaipur

FIG. 8
Jaisalmer *haveli* with pierced sun and moon symbols, Rajasthan, 18th century

FIG. 9
Facade with *bangla* eaves and
*jali*s, Jaisalmer Fort, Rajasthan,
18th century

The medieval city and fortress of Jaisalmer feature elaborate perforated screens carved in the typical golden stone of the region (fig. 9) which provide relief from the fierce sun of the desert. A dazzling play of geometrical patterns creates a filigree facade through which women of the court would have gazed out. A central open balcony allows for a space where a royal male figure could be seated, as depicted in paintings (see fig. 3).[5]

At Deeg, under Jat patronage in the Bharatpur region, a waterside pleasure palace is decorated with pierced walls and railings (figs 10, 11). Structures in and around the same site also incorporate earlier Mughal *jali*s in red sandstone (fig. 12), which stand out against the buff local materials. Later *jali*s are much less fine (figs 13, 14) but cheerfully present nevertheless in this site, which is an odd mix of architectural elements.

FIG. 10

FIG. 11

FIG. 10
Summer Palace, Deeg, Rajasthan,
18th century

FIG. 11
Railing detail, Summer Palace,
Deeg, 18th century

FIG. 12
Back facade wall incorporating
17th-century Mughal *jali*s, Sitaram
temple, Kaman, Rajasthan

FIGs 13 & 14
Two *jali*s from Deeg, late
18th century

FIG. 12

FIG. 13

FIG. 14

FIG. 15

FIGs 15 & 16
Jali bench, Bari, Rajasthan, 19th or early 20th century

'*Jali* mania' is the spirit at nearby Bari where a whimsical sandstone *jali* bench (figs 15, 16) incorporates volutes and flowers and geometric interlace designed to amuse an imaginative patron. In another example of dogged devotion to *jali* designs, a dry and dusty Indian village landscape is seen through a long and lonely

FIG. 16

pierced wall at Chunar (fig. 17). Likely to be fairly modern, its kaleidoscopic designs are centred on floral heads and medallions and reflect the rich carving styles of the nearby historic Chunar fort.

FOLLOWING PAGES
FIG. 17
Landscape with *jali* wall, Chunar, Rajasthan

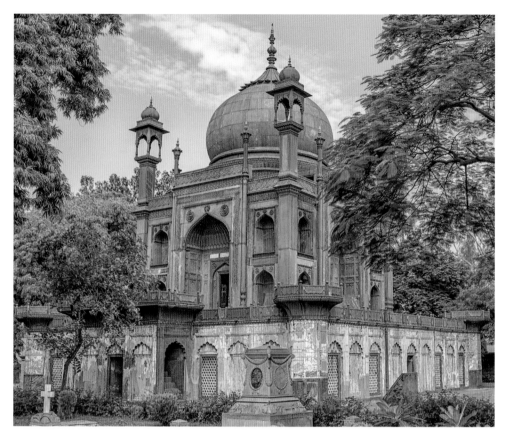

FIG. 18

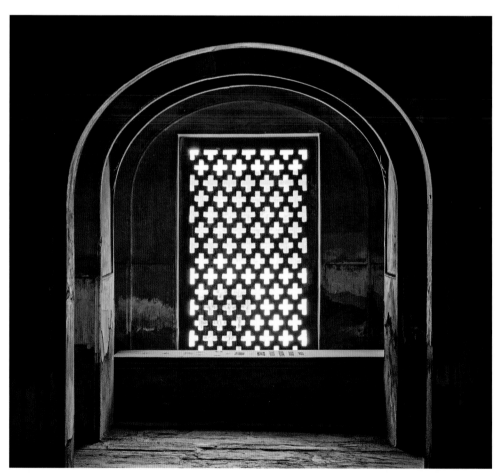

FIG. 18
Mausoleum of Colonel John
William Hessing, Agra,
Uttar Pradesh, c. 1803

FIG. 19
Interior view of one of the
cruciform *jali* screens at
Col. Hessing's mausoleum

FIG. 19

FIG. 20

European interventions on the production of the *jali* screen in northern India can be seen at the Christian cemetery in Agra. Here lies the mausoleum of Dutch military officer Colonel John William Hessing (1709–1803)—the so-called Red Taj Mahal—erected after his death by his widow. Hessing at the time was Commandant of the Agra Fort in charge of the Maratha forces and lost his life in the British capture of Agra in 1803. While the tomb itself imitates the form of the Taj Mahal, it sits on a tall plinth pierced by a series of sixteen *jali* screens, four on each side (fig. 18). These bear a simple repeating pattern of a quatrefoil cross (fig. 19), one of the few stylistic nods to the Christian identity of this otherwise Mughal-style building.

The incorporation of tall and prominent *jali*s in the Victoria College building at Gwalior represents a new development in the colonial-era architecture of the city and in the Indo-Saracenic style more broadly. Designed by British engineer GST Harris (1852–1930) and opened at the end of 1899, the building features a generous and elaborate design for the education and housing of over two-hundred students. The entire edifice is enveloped in a double-storey *jali* veranda surrounding the building. Harris's design drew inspiration from the *jali*s of the local tomb of Muhammad Ghaus in the creation of this pierced outer casing. However, where the tomb of the saint featured a square-grid *jali* design harking back to Sultanate models, Harris's *jali*s incorporate stars, hexagons and ogival trellises of Mughal inspiration (fig. 20), likely reflecting the living traditions of the Gwalior craftsmen, of whom contemporary sources have made mention.[6]

FIG. 20
Screens and carvings, Victoria College, designed by GST Harris, Gwalior, Madhya Pradesh, 1899

FIG. 21

FIG. 22

FIG. 23

FIGs 21, 22, 23 & 24
Jali screen, Rashtrapati Bhavan,
New Delhi, completed 1929

FIG. 25
Exterior facade, Royal Pavilion,
Brighton, completed 1893

Over time, it was the British who became sequestered behind the *jali*. The development of an Indo-Saracenic style of architecture incorporated a grand use of carved and pierced screens. 'Rajput-inspired' *jali*s were incorporated in the Viceroy's House (now the Rashtrapati Bhavan) (figs 21–24) as part of Edwin Lutyens's carefully chosen artistic language for this prestigious and symbolic site, along with other motifs and styles of Indian art and architecture.[7] These merged with European volutes and lyres to form new styles of *jali*. Further away in England, pierced lattice work was inventively adapted by John Nash for the arches on the Indo-Islamic style exterior (fig. 25) of the Royal Pavilion at Brighton, although he never visited India to see the original styles of this feature.

The formula of a simplified trellis within an arch became popular in the buildings of nineteenth- and twentieth-century India. These traditional yet forward-looking designs set the stage for the modernism that was to follow in Indian and global architecture, and still retained something of the romance of the Mughal *jali*. ⊗

FIG. 25

NOTES

1. Goswamy with Bhatia, *The Mandi Bhagavata*, painting: *King Kamsa instructs his confidants*, leaf from a Bhagavata Purana series.

2. Farooq, "Wood and Brick Architecture in Kashmir," 865–74.

3. Golombek, "The Draped Universe of Islam," 25–50; More recently this topic has been discussed in Bush, *Reframing the Alhambra*, 178–180; Clevenot, *Ornament and Decoration* discusses the concepts of the hidden and the seen in "Aesthetics of the Veil," 208.

4. An example may be found in the Museum of Art and Design, Bangalore, Acc. No. TXT.00621.

5. Mehta, *Waseem Ahmed*, 2017. The representation of the human figure seen through a patterned translucent cloth evokes the metaphorical potential of a *jali* textile. As society wrestles with issues of artistic freedom, censorship and the status of women, Lahore-trained miniature painter Waseem Ahmed (b. 1976, Pakistan) opens up the discussion around those issues. He has created an 'Odalisque' reclining nude wearing a translucent burqa, provoking questions about the veiling and viewing of the feminine form.

6. Tillotson, G, "George S. T. Harris: An architect in Gwalior," 13–14.

7. Nath and Mehra, *Dome over India*.

The *Jali* Tradition
Master Craftsmanship and Patronage

Mitchell Abdul Karim Crites

The twentieth century in India began with an architectural project of imperial scale that heralded a remarkable revival of the millennia-old Indian tradition of working with stone. Emperor George V laid the foundation plaque in 1911 for the construction of the new capital of British India on the Ridge, later moved to a small hillock in central Delhi, nestled among the imposing monuments of Sultanate and Mughal India. As the soaring Viceregal Palace, the two imposing Secretariats and the residential and commercial centres began to take form over the next two decades, it became clear that the formidable legacy of design and craftsmanship that could be traced back to the Hindu, Buddhist, Rajput, Sultanate and Mughal architectural traditions weighed heavily on the two chief architects of the project, Edwin Lutyens and Herbert Baker. It was, therefore, essential that New Delhi, the ninth in a series of royal capitals, had to present a symbolic and architectural statement that would stand the test of time.

The legendary quarries of Rajasthan, slumbering for centuries, were remobilized in order to finish the project on schedule and soon tonnes of mottled red sandstone from Tantpura and white marble from Makrana began arriving in Delhi, transported this time not by bullock and elephant, but by train and truck. These were the same quarries from which Emperor Akbar had ordered the sandstone for Fatehpur Sikri and his grandson, Shah Jahan, the marble for the Taj Mahal. *Ustad*s, traditional master stone carvers, in their hundreds, were also recruited to Delhi from the northern Indian states of Uttar Pradesh and Rajasthan to work *in situ* on the acres of carved relief panels, *jali* screens, ornamental railings and floor and wall cladding needed to construct the new capital.

The syncretistic style of design and ornament developed by Lutyens and Baker was highly stylized and a little stiff, and it did not do justice to the incredible skill that still resided in the hands of the *ustad* master carvers. However, the very act of creating a completely new city on such a monumental scale clearly demonstrated that the quarries of the past could be brought back to life and that skilled labour remained abundantly available. It was, however, not until a few decades later

PREVIOUS PAGES
Master craftsman Ramawtar carving white marble, Jaipur, Rajasthan (Frozen Music atelier)

FACING PAGE
Panels at the Shangri La Jali Pavilion Courtesy of the Doris Duke Foundation for Islamic Art, Honolulu, Hawaii (Photo: David Franzen, 2020)

that a striking resurgence of the finest classical traditions of Mughal stone carving and hard stone inlay would take place, demonstrating conclusively that these precious skills were indeed alive and well and would continue till the present day (see pp. 224–225).

❖ Revival of Patronage

Doris Duke, an American heiress to a vast family fortune, married James Cromwell on February 13, 1935 and the couple immediately set off on a ten-month honeymoon tour, starting from Cairo and ending in Tokyo, motivated and guided by her abiding interest in Islamic and Mughal art and architecture. Soon after arriving in India in early March, the couple decided to make a trip by train to Wardha in central India to visit Mahatma Gandhi at his ashram, the All-India Village Industries Association. During a private interview, Gandhi shared his deeply felt conviction that by reviving and supporting the traditional arts and crafts of India, the rural and urban poor could become more prosperous and self-sustaining.

FIG. 1
Doris Duke and James Cromwell
at the Shangri La Jali Pavilion,
Honolulu, 1935
Courtesy of the Doris Duke
Foundation for Islamic Art,
Honolulu, Hawaii

Clearly moved and inspired by Gandhi's vision, the couple returned to Delhi where they continued their tour visiting important Sultanate and Mughal monuments. It was, however, their visit to Agra which seemed to have had the greatest impact on both of them. The exquisite marble carvings and precious stone inlay that they saw at the Taj Mahal and other Mughal monuments impressed the couple greatly. They were also captivated by a visit to one of the finest ateliers in the city, the Indian Marble Works, overseen by Rai Bahadur Seth Lachhman Das, whose family had lived and worked in the heart of old Agra for generations. Many of the *ustad* master carvers and inlay artisans here could themselves trace their ancestry back to the same families who created the Taj Mahal and other Mughal monuments centuries before.

Inspired by the extraordinary craftsmanship that could still be done, Duke returned to Delhi from Agra and made the decision to create a suite of rooms in classical Mughal style for her Palm Beach home. However, once back in the United States at the end of the world tour, the plans changed and she decided to build a completely new home in Honolulu to be christened Shangri La. This elegant and palatial retreat would ultimately incorporate the new marble carving and inlay from Agra along with a significant number of major Islamic and Mughal works of art and architectural elements which the couple had collected during their travels.[1]

While in Delhi, Duke commissioned the British architect Francis Barrington Blomfield to design what is now called the 'Mughal Suite' for the Shangri La bathroom. Along with Blomfield, she and her husband personally selected details from classical Mughal carving, inlay and *jali* screens which they especially admired and wanted to be included in the overall design concept. The wall panels were to be inlaid with precious stone in a series of flowering plants (Fig. 2), inspired by the inlaid walls of the imperial *hammam* inside the Delhi Red Fort. One striking *jali* window carved out of white marble for the Shangri La bath deserves special mention for its sensitive blending of the traditional with the contemporary. This *jali*, a masterwork of design and craftsmanship, depicts an elongated lily plant floating on a geometric lattice (Fig. 3), an elegant filter for light and air falling into the marble chamber beyond.

Duke, at the request of her husband, also commissioned a 'Jali Pavilion' (Fig. 1) for the upper roof terrace of Shangri La carved with pure white marble, from the same quarry that Shah Jahan used for the Taj Mahal and with designs inspired directly by the monumental *jali* screens from the tomb of I'timad al-Daula in Agra. With the commissioning of the Mughal Suite and the Jali Pavilion, Duke placed herself firmly in a tradition of grand architectural patronage practised in the Mughal court by Nur Jahan, wife of Jahangir, and Jahanara, the daughter of Shah Jahan, whose

FIG. 2 (FACING PAGE) & FIG. 3
Carved marble *jali* windows
with floral motifs in the Shangri
La Mughal Suite, designed
by C.G. and F.B. Blomfield,
1935–1938, Agra and Delhi
Courtesy of the Doris Duke
Foundation for Islamic Art,
Honolulu, Hawaii (Photo: David
Franzen, 2020)

FIG. 4

FIG. 5

great personal wealth and power also allowed them to commission buildings of extraordinary beauty and sensitivity. Today, the Shangri La Museum of Islamic Art, Culture & Design is open to the public, a vivid testimony to the inspired eye of a remarkable patron who not only collected but also revived endangered art and craft traditions.

A few decades later, another American patron of the arts appeared and he, too, shared Doris Duke's fascination with the *jali* as an art form. This was Stuart Cary Welch, a gifted scholar, collector, connoisseur of art and under whose tenure as senior consultant of the Islamic Department at the Metropolitan Museum of Art, the ground-breaking INDIA exhibition was inaugurated in 1985. Cary, as he was affectionately called by his friends, students and colleagues, was also one of the first scholars to understand what major works of art Sultanate and Mughal *jali*s truly were.

Over the years, Cary revealed, through his conversations and correspondence with friends and colleagues, his reflections about the possible origin and evolution of the *jali* form. He enjoyed telling the story of how the Prophet Muhammad, while fleeing from his enemies, took refuge in the Cave of Thawr, and how a spider quickly spun its web across the entrance to the cave confounding his attackers into thinking no one was inside. Cary would spin his own story that the spider's web, filtering light and air, could be the origin of the lattice screen so characteristic of Islamic art and architecture and why not, he would say, since the Urdu word *jali* means 'net' or 'web'. Cary would also visualise *jali*s as 'frozen ether' and compare their complex and intricate geometry to the contrapuntal harmonies of a Bach fugue.

While exploring Mughal monuments, which he loved to do, Cary would speculate that the *jali*s found in palaces and tombs commissioned by patrons who were practising Sufis seemed often to have a sense of creative design and beauty that were far ahead of their time. He wondered if they might have been influenced by the esoteric and highly evolved teachings passed on to them by their own Sufi masters. He would often quote the instruction that Dara Shikoh, the son of Shah Jahan, and a great patron of architecture, was given by his spiritual master, Mulla Shah Badakhshi, to create 'lofty buildings, spirit-increasing dwellings and heart-attracting recreation places'.[2]

Over a period of many years, Cary collected a number of important Sultanate and Mughal *jali*s and decided in the late nineties to create his very own 'Jali Mahal', a Palace of Jalis (Fig. 4). It was, of course, an architectural indulgence, but the concept of a freestanding room enclosed by pierced screens placed it securely in the classical Mughal tradition, along with Doris Duke's Jali Pavilion. He even gave

FIG. 4
'Jali Mahal' built by Stuart Cary Welch, New Hampshire

FIG. 5
Stuart Cary Welch at the 'Jali Mahal'

FIG. 6
Cary's Romanesque 'Crucifix Jali',
Jaipur, Rajasthan (Frozen Music
atelier)

FIG. 7

names, 'Big Red' or 'Starry Sky', to his favourite *jali*s. Escaping from the demands of writing or teaching, Cary could often be found reclining on an antique chaise longue in the middle of the Jali Mahal (Fig. 5), listening to classical music, and watching the rays of the sun and moon as they cast ethereal shadows through his beloved *jali*s.

On his many trips to India, Cary always wanted to meet living *ustad*s, master artists and artisans, who could trace their ancestry back to the Mughal courts of Agra, Fatehpur Sikri and Delhi. An accomplished artist himself, he designed two *jali*s which he commissioned to be made by master stone carvers in Jaipur. The 'Crucifix Jali' (Fig. 6) inspired by Romanesque crosses was carved at the Frozen Music workshop in Jaipur, under the sensitive direction of Varun Seth, one of the few cultural revivalists in India who has been able to reinvigorate and maintain traditional Mughal craftsmanship at the highest level.

During one visit to Jaipur in 2003, Cary stayed for a week in a small boutique hotel where he sat on the grassy lawn with two master carvers from the village of Sikandra, near Jaipur, and patiently guided them how to interpret the 'squiggly *jali*' design (Fig. 7), as he called it, that he had sketched the night before. Occasionally, he would take the hammer and chisel himself and chip away the marble to show them the exact play of light and form he wanted. Cary passed away in 2008 and this line from one of the many eloquent tributes that were written at the time sums up the essence of his most remarkable life and legacy: 'He recognised aesthetic qualities in almost everything he saw and brought art to life for others to enjoy.'

Doris Duke and Stuart Cary Welch were far ahead of their time in recognizing the power and beauty of the *jali* form, but even more so in their role of sensitive patrons who were committed to reviving these endangered art and craft traditions and, in the process, ensuring that they would be passed on to future generations.

FIG. 7
Cary's 'Squiggly Jali', Jaipur, Rajasthan (Frozen Music atelier)

❖ The Jali in Daily Life and Worship

We conclude with examples of how the *jali* form continues to be part and parcel of daily life and ritual ceremony in modern-day India. In some ways, these followed in the footsteps of the late nineteenth-century American designer and connoisseur Lockwood de Forest who assembled a collection of pierced brass plaques for furniture decoration from Ahmedabad (Fig. 8), which form a great resource today.

Medanta – The Medicity Hospital located in Gurgaon, now known as Gurugram, is one of the major medical centres servicing Delhi and the national capital region. Visitors and patients entering the lobby are immediately struck by a pair of twenty-one-foot high beige sandstone *jali*s, each carved with a towering tree of life inhabited by birds and forest creatures. The design concept and symbolism of the installation was conceived by Madhu Trehan, a journalist and author of singular sensitivity, who recognized that the centuries-old act of tying cotton strands onto *jali* screens can be in itself an act of worship, meditation and healing. Throughout the day and night, hundreds of patients and their families, while awaiting treatment, take threads from a marble bowl inscribed with the words 'Every Life is Priceless' and tie them directly onto the *jali*s, each one absorbed in their own thoughts and prayers.

For centuries, during the hot months of summer a remarkable act of traditional creativity and ritual devotion has taken place inside the Shri Radha Raman Temple on the banks of the Yamuna river in the ancient town of Vrindavan. Each day, the symbolic dwelling of Lord Krishna, the *Phool Bangla* or House of Flowers (Fig. 9), is erected anew out of white *bela* blossoms which appear only at this time of year. The delicate floral latticework, echoing the geometry of Mughal *jali*s, brings together the vibrant and timeless cultural traditions of two communities who have lived side by side for generations. ⊗

FIG. 8
Cutout by Lockwood de Forest,
Ahmedabad, Gujarat, brass, chased
work, c. 1892,
133 cm (5 1/4 in.) x 210 mm (8 1/4 in.)
The Metropolitan Museum of Art
Gift of Frank and Patricia Goss, 2014
Accession Number: 2014.680.1

FOLLOWING PAGES
FIG. 9
The *Phool Bangla*, a *jali* made
of fresh white jasmine buds, Shri
Radha Raman Temple, Vrindavan,
Uttar Pradesh

NOTES

1. I am deeply indebted to the ground-breaking research done by Dr. Thalia Kennedy on Doris Duke's trip to India and her ordering of the Mughal architectural features for Shangri La. See bibliography.

2. Stuart Cary Welch's comments and thoughts on Mughal *jali* screens were drawn from our correspondence and animated conversations over the years as well as from several legendary excursions with Cary and his beloved wife, Edith, into the heartland of Mughal and Rajput India.

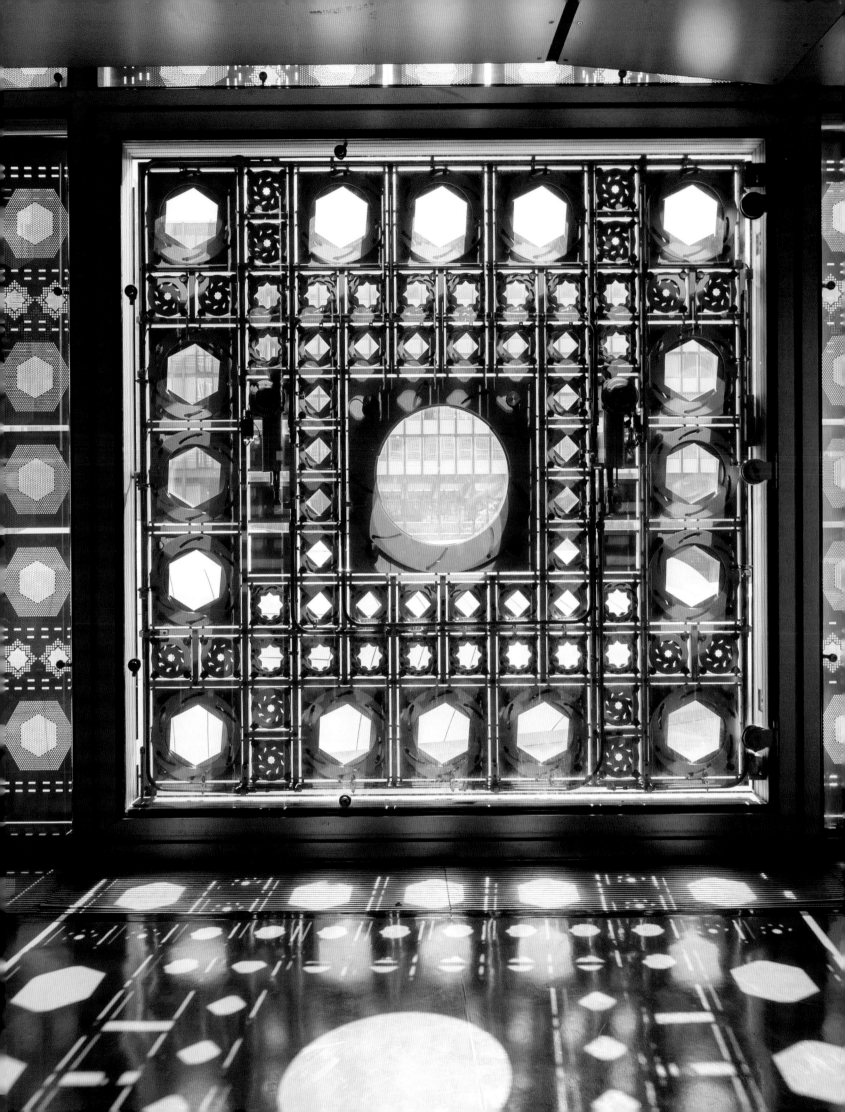

Jali in the Modern Age

"You know the reason I love the stars is because we can't hurt them: we can't burn them, we can't melt them, we can't make them overflow, we can't flood them or blow them up—so we keep reaching for them."

Laurie Anderson, 2010

The modern era has witnessed the reinvigoration of the *jali* form in the hands of new generations of architects and designers. The metaphoric potential of stars and solar symbols, silhouette, shadow, geometric pattern and light reflect the ideas of individual creators, often in response to a world besieged with social, environmental and political challenges. Innovations in materials and technologies bring fresh possibilities for buildings and their functional and decorative features. At the same time, modern art movements have liberated the *jali* from the architectural setting and reinterpreted it as a free style of creative expression.

Following the independence of India in 1947, the language of modernism was embraced in the art and architectural styles of the newly-established democratic republic. This international movement, which originated in the West, was based in part on a philosophy of egalitarianism, utilizing industrially produced and affordable materials to create structures based mainly on function. Modernism by and large rejected ornament, and this had profound implications for traditional Indian craftsmen who had for centuries cut and carved stone, wood and plaster for the decoration of buildings. Many forms of ornament such as relief carving, plaster and gesso decoration, wall painting and traditional *jali* work largely came to an end, minimally sustained by government-supported guilds for the preservation of historical monuments or by a few private patrons, such as former royal families in order to maintain their historical properties. Despite these wide-reaching changes in patronage and style, the *jali* did not completely disappear, but became reinterpreted and simplified as a feature of modernist architecture in materials such as glazed ceramic, baked brick and even exposed concrete. In South Asia, the reason for its survival was likely as much

FACING PAGE
Metallic *mashribiyya* screen, Institut du Monde Arabe, Paris, France, 1987
Architects: Jean Nouvel, Architecture Studio, Gilbert Lèzenes, Pierre Soria

FIG. 1

FIG. 2

FIG. 3

FIG. 4

FIG. 5

practical as decorative since the *jali*, along with the *chhajja* (a protruding sunshade built over windows on the exterior of a building), continues to protect modern spaces from the heat and glare of the Indian sun. This also demonstrates the evolution of modernism as it grew beyond its Western origins, incorporating features, techniques and functions from non-Western contexts.

Under the so-called International Style, a subset to modernism that had developed in Europe in the early part of the twentieth century, a 'straightforward' approach to buildings took hold, particularly symbolic of American power and practicality. The iconic US Chancery building in New Delhi built in the 1950s and designed by architect Edward Durell Stone (1902–78) stands as a large, clean box on a podium, protected by a surrounding exterior curtain wall of pierced sun-screen or *jali* (fig. 1). Consisting of circles set into a square grid, the screen provided ornamental relief to the otherwise spare lines of the building. This same pattern was utilized by the architect in several US projects, including the grille-work facade in his 1956 New York town house where it was a somewhat controversial addition to the Upper East Side. While the diaper pattern is said to have been Stone's response to Indian *jali*s, it is also reflective of the simple and repetitive forms favoured by the International Style.

FIG. 1
Chancery Building, Embassy of the United States of America, New Delhi, 1959
Architect: Edward Durell Stone

FIG. 2
India International Centre, New Delhi, 1962
Architect: Joseph Allen Stein

FIG. 3
'Delhi blue' ceramic *jali* (detail), India International Centre, New Delhi

FIG. 4
Ceramic window *jali* with abstract Kufic design, 18th–19th century
Private collection, Hong Kong

FIG. 5
Ceramic window *jali* from a Sikh shrine, 18th–19th century
Private collection, Hong Kong

While the US Chancery's monumental *jali*s were cast in concrete, more delicate 'Delhi blue' glazed *jali*s appear in the contemporary work of India-based American architect Joseph Allen Stein (1912–2001). The India International Centre in New Delhi, an important social, diplomatic and residential establishment, was inaugurated in 1962 (fig. 2). In the words of Stein, "...it is a place where a certain kind of relationship exists—between the garden and the building and the water and earth and the sky."[1] This sense of porousness to the building is achieved by its facades which essentially take the form of long geometrically-pierced curved screens that let in light and views while providing shade. Vivid turquoise blue glazed terracotta *jali*s in scallop patterns are incorporated in areas of this outward facing grille (fig. 3), sometimes acting as separators between guest rooms. These tiles bring colour to the muted tonalities of the modernist structure while also harmonizing with the overall pierced appearance and scalloped roofing detail.

Applied glazed ceramic tile-work is well known in earlier Sultanate and Mughal buildings such as in the *madrasa* of Mahmud Gawan in Bidar or on the *chhatri* pavilions in Humayan's Tomb, Delhi, although pierced *jali* screens are less common in that medium. A hexagonal tiled *jali* window with floral border from the Lattan Masjid (1493–1519) in Gaur is a rare survivor of the style.[2] Glazed ceramic *jali*s remained in use through the eighteenth and nineteenth centuries. Two green glazed *jali*s from this period offer different designs within arched profiles. A dark green example of brighter hue from a set of *roshandaan*s (ventilation windows), placed high to let in light, contains a geometric pattern evoking abstract Kufic calligraphy (fig. 4). The other, with a stylized plant, comes from a Sikh shrine in Punjab (fig. 5). This ceramic production continued through the twentieth century and laid the foundation for the distinctive 'Delhi blue' *jali* work, which became quite widely seen in the modernist architecture of the '50s.

The Delhi-based architect Habib Rahman (1915–95) saw the *jali* element as among the key features of the liberation of Indian modernist architecture from that of the West: "Rabindra Bhavan, which was nominated for the Aga Khan award in 1980, was the first building where I could free myself from the influence of Walter Gropius and Oscar Niemeyer. This building belonged to India. Here, I have used traditional Indian elements such as *chhajja*s, *jali*s and overhanging roofs. It was the first functional building to give me aesthetic satisfaction."[3] Rahman's Rabindra Bhavan complex (1961), built to house the three national academies, integrated flattened blocks of stone, stone *jali*s and concrete details together with other elements to create a site where traditional and modern elements coexisted. The *jali*s were a prominent feature, incorporating new and existing geometric designs in densely screened facades. Rahman's later tomb memorial of Fakhruddin Ali Ahmed, a former President of India, constructed in 1975

FIG. 6

FIG. 7

near the Parliament House in the heart of the city, offers a simplified interpretation of the long-standing tradition of South Asian funerary architecture (fig. 6). This elegant structure, outlined by white marble screens and arches, is open to the air and sky, referencing the Sufi tradition of an open-air tomb. The cenotaph rests on a low, octagonal plinth, surrounded by four open arches with alternating *jali* walls. The *jalis* feature overlapping *mihrab* shapes and oblong cartouches, interspersed with illusory six-pointed stars. Freed from a structural wall setting, the architect's aim to draw open, linear forms becomes apparent. With graphic clarity, the arches and geometry echo the features of a nearby Mughal-period mosque.

The ambition to create an entire building as a monumental three-dimensional *jali* was asserted by Raj Rewal (b. 1934) in his Hall of Nations pavilion (fig. 7), inaugurated in New Delhi in 1972 as part of the Pragati Maidan exhibition complex. Described as a 'Brutalist masterpiece', the building, structurally engineered by Mahendra Raj as one of the world's largest wide-span works in reinforced concrete, was demolished in 2017 in the face of an international outcry.[4] Rewal described his vision for the Hall of Nations as stemming from his interest in structure and weave forms in nature and traditional architecture, its form "based on tetrahedrons, triangulated forms, hexagons—these are very much seen in almost any *jalis*, so these were three-dimensional *jalis*".[5] He saw the structure itself as integrating the elements of a *brise soleil* or sun-breaker to create a shaded interior of diffused light.

FIG. 6
Tomb of Fakhruddin Ali Ahmed,
New Delhi, 1975
Architect: Habib Rahman

FIG. 7
Hall of Nations, New Delhi, 1972
Architect: Raj Rewal

FIG. 8

FIG. 9

The skilful laying of exposed brick provides another means to bring about *jali* effects in modern Indian buildings. Openwork brick patterns are seen as a signature style of the facades of the Thiruvananthapuram-based architect and Gandhian Laurie Baker. His ecologically responsible and low-cost structures were frequently constructed in baked brick, using techniques and formats to bring light and air into organically-shaped spaces and structures. The distinctive spiral-shaped India Coffee House (1958) with pierced walls (fig. 8) and inventively conceived Centre for Development Studies (1971) outside Thiruvananthapuram (fig. 9) are two celebrated examples of his visionary style. In particular, he used the idea of a surrounding *jali* wall, or skin, to act as both an aesthetic feature and also a cooling device for the inner structure. Baker's repertoire of shaped openings includes pairs of stepped triangles, ziggurat profiles and cross patterns. Some of these shapes echo medieval Persian baked brick designs (fig. 10), including simple cross patterns. A more recent example of pierced brickwork can be seen in the Bait ur-Rouf Mosque (fig. 11) designed by Bangladeshi architect Marina Tabassum, winner of the Aga Khan Award for Architecture in 2016. Set in an economically challenged neighbourhood of Dhaka, this deceptively simple rectangular structure makes striking aesthetic and atmospheric statements through its bastions and corner facades where the bricks are laid in an openwork grid to create an interior space dappled with symmetrical rays of light. A flat dome ceiling at the centre of the building is pierced with small openings that draw further beams of light into the chamber below.

FIG. 10

FIG. 11

FIG. 12

FIG. 12
Louvre Abu Dhabi, UAE, founded
2007
Architect: Jean Nouvel

FIG. 13
Aga Khan Museum, Toronto,
Canada, 2014
Architect: Fumihiko Maki / Maki and
Associates

New materials and forms of engineering have allowed for fresh possibilities for the *jali* in global architecture, pushing frontiers in the use of metal towards the creation of a moving, pierced surface. Constructed in the 1980s by architect Jean Nouvel, the Institut du Monde Arabe in Paris broke new ground by imagining the exterior as a movable and changeable rectangular screen wall of ocular geometric openings that could open or close through a mechanical louvre system (see p. 240). This *brise soleil* regulates the light within the interior while creating 240 metallic *mashribiyya*s on the south facade. In a more recent project by the same architect metallic materials are used to innovate further new effects. The recently completed site of the Louvre Abu Dhabi, UAE, designed by Ateliers Jean Nouvel, takes inspiration from the *medina* (meaning 'city' in Arabic) and low-lying Arab settlements to create 55 small buildings surmounted by a vast dome pierced with 7850 stars, each one unique in form (fig. 12). The structure is created by eight different openwork layers in steel and aluminium through which rays of light are filtered before appearing and then disappearing in the space below. The result is a cinematic effect, named the 'rain of light', as the sun travels through the day.[6] The multiple layers of the roof carve the

FIG. 13

light into almost visibly moving projections on the ground below. This 'cartography' is designed so that the luminosity interacts with the dust in the air and the reflection of the pools of water in the space and distributes it appropriately for the galleries below.[7] The asymmetrical layout of the stars and their varying shapes mark a departure from the formal and measured layouts of Islamic architecture, yet the domed interior with starry piercings references that heritage. Taking full advantage of new materials and algorithms to effectuate maximum capability, the structural engineering of the roof reflects the new technologies available to the twenty-first-century architect. The dome has become an iconic feature of Abu Dhabi, capturing the aspirations of the Gulf state to win its place in the contemporary cultural world.

The advances in modern glass technologies offer yet another material for architects experimenting with new expressions of filtered light. An ethereal central court framed by lacy *mashribiyya*s etched on glass walls (fig. 13) forms the heart of the Aga Khan Museum in Toronto, built in 2014. The museum building, designed by Japanese architect Fumihiko Maki, together with the Ismaili Centre designed by Charles Correa and Formal Gardens by Vladimir Djurovic occupy a 16-acre site. The inspiration of light has dictated much of the design of the museum space, including filigree patterns which reference historical and geographic elements of the museum's art collections. The courtyard is intended as 'a permanent peaceful sanctuary creating its own internal world secluded from the outside environment. Its glass walls are imprinted with a double layered pattern in line and void to create a three-dimensional effect recalling the traditional Islamic *jali* screens.'[8] These starry patterns of the semi-transparent walls shimmer along the interior galleries that define the courtyard space.

❖ Art and Design

*Jali*s once freed from the context of buildings take on independent modes of expression that often have little to do with architecture but expand the possibilities of the interplay of light and silhouette as they push into new conceptual spaces. When considered together it becomes apparent that the visual language of the *jali* lends itself to several unifying themes in the work of modern and contemporary artists. The discourses surrounding such material provoke intellectual and theoretical questions as much as discussions of form. Women artists in particular have claimed space in front of the pierced screen rather than behind it, challenging gender norms and established patriarchies in this respect.

Grid or geometric forms are used by the London-based British-Palestinian artist Mona Hatoum (b. 1952, Beirut) to reference systems of control within society. Her body of work includes installation and sculpture executed in a wide range of materials. Hatoum's dramatic installation *Light Sentence*, created in 1992 out of stacked wire-mesh lockers illuminated by a slow-moving motorized light bulb, casts shadows of harsh and unsettling memory rooted in personal battles with disorientation, displacement and identity (fig. 14). Here, the *jali* has become a cage, and the light appears as a spirit, trapped within. Hatoum eschews a simplistic connection between her personal narrative and visual expression, saying, "Often the work is about conflict and contradiction—and that conflict or contradiction can be within the actual object."[9]

The experience of exile and themes of social justice are also explored by Afruz Amighi (b. 1974, Tehran), a US-based sculptor and installation artist. *Still Garden*, created in 2011, is formed by the projection of light through a hand-cut sheet of woven polyethylene (fig. 15), the same material used to construct refugee tents. Amighi uses vegetal and geometric patterns and also integrates references to Persian painting. Among them are images of crowns and serpents—an allusion to the evil figure of Zahhak in the Persian national epic, the *Shahnama* of Firdausi. Shackled birds and bouquets of flowers present further nuanced commentary on Middle Eastern current affairs. An almost opposite effect—one of contemplativeness—is

FIG. 14

seen in a 2013 installation *Intersections* (fig. 16) by Pakistani-American artist Anila Quayyum Agha (b. 1965). A single light bulb inside a large, suspended metal cube laser-cut with geometry inspired from the Alhambra bathes the walls, ceiling and floor of the chamber with waves of interlacing pattern, enveloping all who enter this transcendental space. This visual strategy has been employed by the artist in several other works, creating a body of material that explores the range of meanings and possibilities afforded by different patterns and colours created in this way.

Open-air pierced walls set in public spaces appear in the works of multidisciplinary artist Nevin Aladag (b. 1972, Turkey) and sculptor Hector Zamora (b. 1974, Mexico). The artists approach the expressive possibilities of a porous wall from very different traditions and with varying aims. Aladag's 2016 outdoor installation in Vienna titled *Screens I–III* consisted of three large freestanding screens erected on a pedestrian street (fig. 17). The screens were created with roughly-finished cuboid cobblestones of granite and marble laced through metal rods to form geometric patterns, evoking

FIG. 14
Light Sentence, 1992
Mona Hatoum
Wire mesh lockers, slow-moving
motorized light bulb

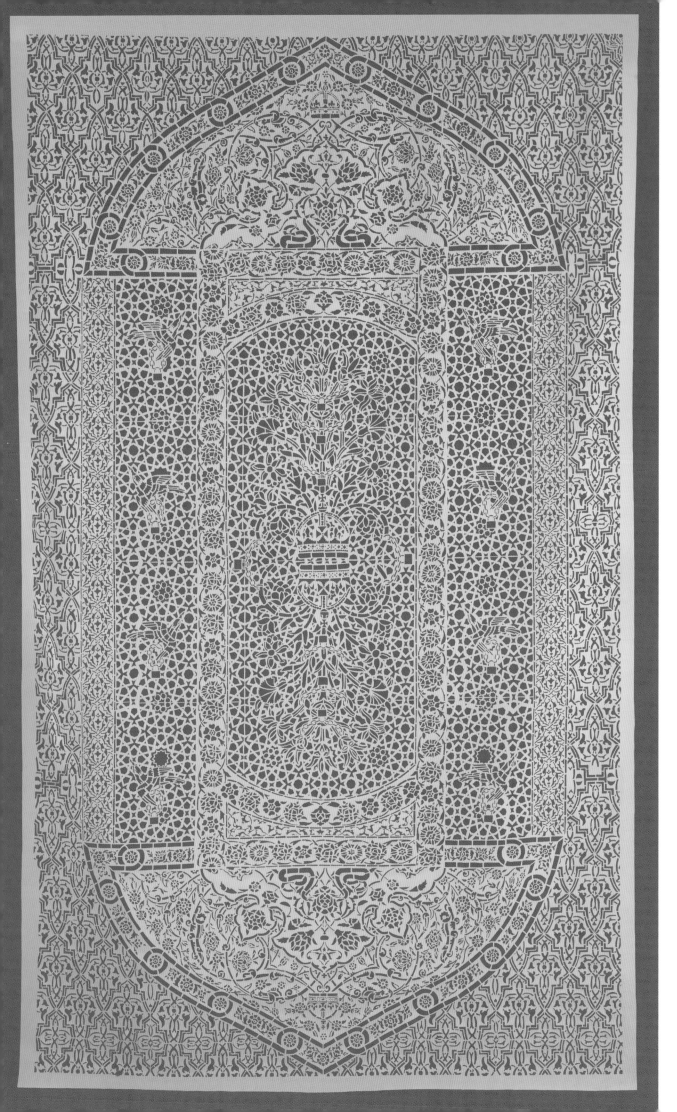

FIG. 16

semi-transparent ornamental *mashribiyya*s as well as referencing the historical contexts of local conflict in which those same materials were used. Zamora's monumental rooftop installation *Lattice Detour*, commissioned by the Metropolitan Museum in 2020, employs traditional hollow baked bricks to create a see-through wall, pixilating the view of Central Park and creating both separation and connection (fig. 18). Referencing the US debate around the proposal of a dividing southern border wall, Zamora's work was topical to the political issues of the moment. His pierced and porous wall makes a contemporary statement on multiple ways of looking at and through a symbol of social and political division. In a different mood is Tarik Currimbhoy's sculptural creation *Circular Fused Jalis* (fig. 19), exploring the effect of focused piercings in a large plane, echoing the circularity of the whole. It is created by using the forces of balance and compression in high-contrast materials.

FACING PAGE
FIG. 15
Still Garden, 2011
Afruz Amighi
Woven polyethylene, plexiglass
The Metropolitan Museum of Art
Purchase, 2011 NoRuz at The Met
Benefit, 2011
Accession Number: 2011.427

FIG. 16
Intersections, 2013
Anila Qayyum Agha
Laser cut and painted wood

FIG. 17

FIG. 18

FIG. 19

FIG. 17
Screens I–III, 2016
Nevin Aladag
Cobblestones, steel frames,
stainless steel grid, Installation,
Kunstplatz Graben, Vienna, Austria
(Photo by Iris Ranziger)

FIG. 18
Lattice Detour, 2020
Hector Zamora
Terracotta brick

FIG. 19
*Circular Fused Jali*s, 2021
Tarik Currimbhoy
Stainless steel
Courtesy: Ann Norton Sculpture
Gardens

FIG. 20

The traditional wooden *mashribiyya* lattice screens, so symptomatic of many parts of the Islamic world, are made with carved and turned wooden elements that meet and lock around larger, rounded nuggets. Like Mughal *jali*s, they also provide shade and privacy and have evolved, over time, from an aesthetic sensitivity to the effects of light and pattern. Aside from the buildings of Cairo or Damascus, such screens are also found in the domestic structures in the cities of Mecca, Medina and Jeddah. The Egyptian–German visual artist Susan Hefuna (b.1962) draws vivid references from *mashribiyya* screens while, at the same time, integrating elements of Arabic text into the design, which she describes as "coding and decoding the different layers of viewing in different cultural contexts". In her graphic work *Ehna* (Us), she presents a bold wooden lattice constructed out of a regular grid of squares with the calligraphy balanced strategically on the ledge of an open central space framed by vertical lines (fig. 20). A monumental wooden screen, created for the Islamic galleries at the British Museum by Ahmad Angawi (b. 1981), references the geometric *mangour* style of the Hijaz (fig. 21). The Saudi artist, designer and cultural revivalist works closely with master woodcarvers and artisans, having been motivated from a young age by the groundbreaking studies of the architecture of early Mecca, Medina and Jeddah conducted by his father, noted scholar and architect Dr. Sami Angawi. The *mangour* interlocking system is self–sufficient in that it holds together without the use of nails or glue. Angawi often acknowledges his design work as being guided by the fundamental Islamic concept of *al-mizan*, which stresses balance as a state of mind.

Two-dimensional works on paper explore the potential of the *jali* through the medium of graphic expression. A collage created in 2017 by the artist and printmaker Zarina Hashmi (1937–2020) is a design for a *jali* screen made for a building in Hyderabad (fig. 22). This strongly graphic work presents a series of registers that evoke

FIG. 20
Ehna (Us), 2009
Susan Hefuna
Ink on wood

FIG. 21

architectural screens, shuttered windows and abstract blinds, among other patterns. The imagery also integrates many of the themes in Hashmi's wider work, such as hanging light bulbs from the installation *Descending Darkness* and a mobile house from her sculpture series *House on Four Wheels* appearing as dark silhouettes against the light ground. Hashmi's body of work explores features of architecture, citing themes of home, migration and displacement through the construction of conceptual floorplans and abstracted architectural details.

FIG. 22

FIG. 21
Mangour screen, 2017
Ahmad Angawi
Digital and handcrafted wood,
British Museum, London

FIG. 22
Proposed design sketch for
a *jali*, c. 2016
Zarina Hashmi
Collage, New York

FIG. 23

Transcending liminal spaces, a watercolour view of Bethlehem seen through a geometric window grille (fig. 23) is by New York- and Connecticut-based painter James Worth (b. 1933). A deep blue night sky filled with stars—including the flashing North Star—hangs over a hilly vista below in which shepherds tend their flock with a chapel in the distance. The interwoven lines of the stellar pattern of the window trellis are inspired by the design of a Mamluk-period inlay *minbar* door in the collection of the Metropolitan Museum.[10] The interpolation of an Islamicate star screen placed between the viewer and the Biblical landscape in some ways takes the place of the parapet, a space-dividing device that often appears in early images of the Virgin and Child. Where a parapet serves to create two planes, separating the viewer from the view, the window motif here connects them in overlaying levels of symbolism and meaning.

FIG. 24

FIG. 25

The translucency of gems invites *jali*-inspired designs in the jewelled arts, aiming to create air and light around the precious gemstones. A gold, gemstone and white agate brooch (fig. 24) created by Paris-based jewellery designer JAR in 2002 broke new ground in interpreting an architectural motif in precious materials. Of a cusped arch form, the brooch relegates the *jali* effect to the reverse where it appears in interwoven wavy forms. Indian jewellery has long had a tradition of ornamenting hidden surfaces with highly finished designs, perhaps referenced here. In the work of Mumbai-based jeweller Viren Bhagat we encounter another conceptual and technical setting in jewellery that closely conveys the spirit of an architectural *jali*. A diamond brooch created in 2015 is of arched profile with circular, half-moon and pear-shaped diamonds that seemingly float to form an airy surface of light and lustre (fig. 25). ⊗

NOTES

1. India International Centre, https://iicdelhi.in/history.

2. Hasan, *Mosque Architecture of pre-Mughal Bengal*, 119, 123, pl. XXII (b).

3. Rahman, "A tribute: Habib Rahman," 33.

4. Snyder, "The unexpectedly tropical history of Brutalism," August 15, 2019.

5. Rewal, *Indian Modernity*, 2017. Rewal also made use of the *jali* feature in his designs for The Ismaili Center in Lisbon and the Parliament Library in New Delhi.

6. Nouvel, *Global Architecture Document* 145, 33.

7. Ibid, 100. Interview with partner architect Hala Warde explains the planning and making of the dome.

8. "The Aga Khan Museum / Maki and Associates," July 30, 2018.

9. Tate Museum website.

10. Pair of Minbar Doors, Accession Number: 91.1.2064, The Metropolitan Museum of Art, New York.

ntil I first saw with wonder the exquisite white marble pavilions of Agra and Delhi, I had supposed that all, or most, of India's classical architecture consisted of dark layers of stone stacked up, a bit like the stones of the pyramids of Egypt, though unlike those, covered with figures of amorous entwined gods and goddesses. I never imagined the airy lightness of a Mughal palace or tomb, through which breezes can blow as they enter the marble lattices called *jali*s. These have a way of somehow cooling you, even on the most fiery days, and throw complex patterns at your feet, as if you are treading on a floating, ever-changing carpet, laid out for you on a cool stone floor. If you hold your hands out, turning them this way and that, back and forth, the changing patterns can be there too. When you are visiting a tomb, could there ever be a more perfect, beautiful room or space? Who would not like to lie there forever?

When I was shooting the documentary film I was making about Delhi in 1960, I would station myself, setting up my camera, by one of the *jali*s in Shah Jahan's Red Fort palace next to River Yamuna. As tourists moved around beyond it, I would slowly re-focus my camera lens in, then out, then back again, until I had something I liked, some evanescent image that I thought would be useful. I used a lot of my precious sixteen-millimeter colour film doing this; an irresistible pleasure, these images were an effect the eye itself cannot create. The many different colours of women's saris captured through the tracery were especially desirable, fading in, then out, then away, and I used to lie in wait for these women with my camera. Like birdsong, I could hear them coming, chattering away, calling to their children, as I stood ready to turn over within the dappled light of the *jali*.

James Ivory
Film director, writer, photographer

Bibliography

Abbas, Masooma. "Ornamental Jalis of the Mughals and their Precursors." *International Journal of Humanities and Social Science*, vol. 6, no. 3 (March 2016).

Acharya, Prasanna Kumar. *Architecture of Manasara: Translated from Original Sanskrit*, volume 4. New Delhi: Oriental Books Reprint Corporation, 1980.

Alam, Muzaffar. "The Mughals, the Sufi Shaikhs and the Formation of the Akbari Dispensation." *Modern Asian Studies* 43, no. 1 (2009). Accessed June 13, 2020. https://www.jstor.org/stable/20488075?seq=1.

Asher, Catherine. *Architecture of Mughal India*, volume 4, The New Cambridge History of India. Cambridge: Cambridge University Press, 1992.

Barnes, Ruth. *Indian Block-Printed Textiles in Egypt: The Newberry Collection in the Ashmolean Museum, Oxford*, 2 vols. New York: Clarendon Press, 1997.

Behrens-Abouseif, Doris. *Metalwork from the Arab world and the Mediterranean*. London: Thames and Hudson Ltd., 2021.

Bloom, Jonathan and Sheila Blair, eds. *God is the Light of the Heavens and the Earth: Light in Islamic Art and Culture*, The Biennial Hamad bin Khalifa Symposium on Islamic Art. London: Yale University Press, in association with Qatar Foundation, Virginia Commonwealth University, and Virginia Commonwealth University School of the Arts in Qatar, 2015

Bloom, Jonathan M. "The Marble Panels in the Mihrab of the Great Mosque of Kairouan." In *The Aghlabids and Their Neighbors: Art and Material Culture in Ninth-Century North Africa Series*, Handbook of Oriental Studies, Section 1, the Near and Middle East, ed. Glaire D. Anderson, Corisande Fenwick and Mariam Rosser Owen. Leiden and Boston: Brill, 2017. Online publication date: December 12, 2018.

Bonner, Jay. *Islamic Geometric Patterns: Their Historical Development and Traditional Methods of Construction*. New York: Springer, 2017.

Bukhari, Qamoos, (ed.). *Architectural ornamentation in Shrines and Mosques of Kashmir*. New Delhi, Roli Books, 2021

Burgess, JAS. *On the Muhammadan Architecture of Bharoch, Cambay, Dholka, Champanir and Mahmudabad in Gujarat*. London: W. Griggs & Sons, Limited, 1896.

Burton-Page, John. "Sultanate Architecture." In *Indian Islamic Architecture: Forms and Typologies, Sites and Monuments*, edited by Michell George. Leiden and Boston: Brill, 2008.

Bush, Olga. *Reframing the Alhambra: Architecture, Poetry, Textiles and Court Ceremonial*. Edinburgh: Edinburgh University Press, 2018.

Clévenot, Dominique. "Aesthetics of the Veil." In *Ornament and Decoration in Islamic Architecture*. London: Thames & Hudson, 2000.

Cousens, Henry. *BIJAPUR And its Architectural Remains with an Historical Outline of the Adil Shahi Dynasty*. Bombay: Government Central Press, 1916.

Creswell, K. A. C. *A Short Account of Early Muslim Architecture*. Rev. and enl. ed. / revised and supplemented by James W. Allan. Aldershot: Scholar Press, 1989.

Creswell, K. A. C. *Early Muslim Architecture: Vol. 1*. Oxford: Clarendon Press, 1969.

Critchlow, Keith. *Islamic Patterns: An Analytical and Cosmological Approach*. London: Thames and Hudson, 1976.

Dhaky, M. A. *The Indian Temple Traceries*. New Delhi: American Institute of Indian Studies, 2005.

Digby, Simon. "Before Timur Came: Provincialization of the Delhi Sultanate through the Fourteenth Century." *Journal of the Economic and Social History of the Orient* 47, no. 3 (2004). Accessed June 25, 2020. www.jstor.org/stable/25165052.

Dodds, Jerrilynn D., ed. *Al-Andalus: The Art of Islamic Spain* (Exhibition Catalogue). New York: The Metropolitan Museum of Art, 1992.

Ekhtiar, M., P. Soucek, S. Canby and N. Haidar. *Masterpieces from the Department of Islamic Art in the Metropolitan Museum of Art*. New York: The Metropolitan Museum of Art, 2011.

Farooq, Syed Guzanfar. "Wood and Brick Architecture in Kashmir (1339–1585 A.D.): Stylistic, Idiomatic and Axiomorphic Changes." *Proceedings of the Indian History Congress* 74 (2013). http://www.jstor.org/stable/44158888.

Fasih ud-din, Maulvi. *The Sharqi Monuments of Jaunpur*. Badaun, 1922.

Flood, Finbarr Barry. "Before the Mughals: Material Culture of Sultanate North India." *Muqarnas* 36 (2019).

Flood, Finbarr Barry. "The Earliest Islamic Windows as Architectural Decoration." *Persica* 14 (1990–1992).

Flood, Finbarr Barry. "The Flaw in the Carpet: Disjunctive Continuities and Riegl's Arabesque." In *Histories of Ornament: From Global to Local*, edited by Gülru Necipoğlu and Alina Payne. Princeton, N.J.: Princeton University Press, 2016.

Flood, Finbarr Barry. "The Ottoman Windows in the Dome of the Rock and the Aqsa Mosque." In *Ottoman Jerusalem, The Living City: 1517-1917*, edited by Sylvia Auld and Robert Hillenbrand. London: Altajir World of Islam Trust, 2000.

Fogg, Sam. *Red Stone: Indian Stone Carving from Sultanate and Mughal India*. London: Francesca Galloway and Sam Fogg, 2012.

Ghouchani, Abdullah. *Inscriptions on Nishabur Pottery*. Tehran: Reza Abbasi Museum, 1986.

Golombek, L. "The Draped Universe of Islam." In *Content and Context of Visual Arts in the Islamic World*, edited by Priscilla P. Soucek. University Park, P.A. and London: CAA

Goswamy, BN in association with Usha Bhatia. *Ancient Tales of the Lord: Five Leaves from a Bhagavata Purana Series*. Privately printed, 2014.

Grabar, Oleg. *The Mediation of Ornament*. Princeton, N.J.: Princeton University Press, 1992.

Greenwood, William and Lucien de Guise. *Inspired by the East: How the Islamic World Influenced Western Art* (Exhibition Catalogue). London: British Museum, 2019.

Hamdani, Hakim Sameer. *Syncretic traditions of Islamic religious architecture of Kashmir (early 14th-18th century)*. Abingdon, Oxon; New York, NY: Routledge, 2021.

Hamdani, Hakim Sameer. "Understanding Kashmir's Islamic Religious Architecture in Continuity and Change." Qamoos Bukhari (ed.), *Architectural Ornamentation in Shrines and Mosques of Kashmir*. New Delhi, Roli Books, 2021.

Hasan, Syed Mahmadul. *Mosque Architecture of pre-Mughal Bengal*. Bangladesh: University Press Limited, 1979.

Hillenbrand, Robert. *Islamic Architecture: Form, Function, and Meaning*. New York: Columbia University Press, 2004.

Hillenbrand, Robert, "The Uses of Light in Islamic Architecture", In Bloom, Jonathan and Sheila Blair, eds. *God is the Light of the Heavens and the Earth: Light in Islamic Art and Culture*, The Biennial Hamad bin Khalifa Symposium on Islamic Art. London: Yale University Press, in association with Qatar Foundation, Virginia Commonwealth University, and Virginia Commonwealth University School of the Arts in Qatar, 2015

Jain, Jinisha. "Structure as a document." In *Structural Analysis of Historic Construction*, edited by Dina D'Ayala and Enrico Fodde. London: Taylor & Francis Group, 2008.

Kalim, Abu Talib. *Padshahnama*, Persian ms, British Library, Asia, Pacific and Africa Collections, Eth A 1570.

Kachani, Abu Talib Kalim, *Diwan*, Edited by Partau Bezai. Tehran: Kitabfaroshi Khyyam, 1957 (1336).

Kambo, Muhammad Salih. *'Amal-i Salih/Shah Jahannama*, ed. Wahid Quraishi, based on the Calcutta edn of 1912–46 by Ghulam Yazdani, 2nd edn, Lahore: Majlis-i Taraqqi-yi Adab, 1967–72, vol. 1.

Kennedy, Thalia. "Gandhi and Doris Duke: Revitalization of a Crafts Tradition." *Shangri La Working Papers in Islamic Art*, no. 3. Shangri La: A Center for Islamic Arts and Cultures, Honolulu, HI (July 2012).

Khan, Iqtidar Alam. "New Light on the History of Two Early Timurid Monuments of Bayana." *Proceedings of the Indian History Congress* 47 (1986). www.jstor.org/stable/44141557.

Koch, Ebba. "Jahangir as Francis Bacon's Ideal of the King as an Observer and Investigator of Nature". *Journal of the Royal Asiatic Society*, series 3, 19, 3 (2009).

Koch, Ebba. *The Complete Taj Mahal: And the Riverfront Gardens of Agra*. London: Thames & Hudson, 2006 and 2012.

Koch, Ebba. "Mughal Palace Gardens from Babur to Shah Jahan (1526–1648)." *Muqarnas* 14 (1997).

Koch, E. "Influence on Mughal Architecture", in George Michell and Snehal Shah (eds), *Ahmadabad*. Bombay: Marg Publications, 1988

Koch, Ebba. "The Baluster Column – a European Motif in Mughal Architecture and its Meaning." *Journal of the Warburg and Courtauld Institutes*, 1982.

Lambourn, Elizabeth. "A self-conscious art? Seeing Micro-architecture in Sultanate South Asia." *Muqarnas* 27 (2010).

Lambourn, Elizabeth. "Carving and Communities: Marble Carving for Muslim Patrons at Khambhāt and around the Indian Ocean Rim, Late Thirteenth-Mid-Fifteenth Centuries." *Ars Orientalis* 34 (2004).

Lowry, Glenn D. "Humayun's Tomb: Form, Function, and Meaning in Early Mughal Architecture." *Muqarnas* 4 (1987). Accessed May 25, 2020. https://www.jstor.org/stable/1523100.

Mehta, Sage, *Waseem Ahmed*, essay for Jason McCoy gallery, New York, 2017: https://static1. squarespace.com/static/5c6444b9e4afe91469c 174f8/t/5c76afcfc8302509d67a5725/1551282129 684/Waseem_MEHTA_ESSAY.pdf.

Meier, Prita. *Swahili Port Cities: The Architecture of Elsewhere*. Indiana University Press, 2016.

Michell, George. *The Majesty of Mughal Decoration: The Art and Architecture of Islamic India*. London: Thames & Hudson, 2007.

Moynihan, Elizabeth B. *Paradise as a Garden: in Persia and Mughal India*. New York: George Braziller, 1979.

Nath, Aman. *A Dome Over India: Rashtrapati Bhavan*. New Delhi: President's Secretariat; Mumbai, India: India Book House; Woodbridge, Suȷolk, UK; Wappingers' Falls, NY, 2002.

Necipoğlu, Gülru and Alina Payne, eds. *Histories of Ornament: From Global to Local*, Princeton, N.J.: Princeton University Press, 2016.

Necipoğlu, Gülru. "Early Modern Floral: The Agency of Ornament in Ottoman and Safavid Visual Cultures". In Gülru Necipoğlu and Alina Payne (eds), *Histories of Ornament: From Global to Local*, Princeton and Oxford: Princeton University Press, 2016.

Necipoğlu, Gülru. *The Topkapi Scroll: Geometry and Ornament in Islamic Architecture*, Topkapi Palace Museum Library MS H. 1956. Santa Monica: The Getty Center for the History of Art and the Humanities, 1995.

Nouvel, Jean. *Global Architecture Document 145*, Louvre Abu Dhabi, Special Issue, A.D.A. Edita, Tokyo, Japan, February 2018.

Nath, R. *Architecture of Fatehpur Sikri: forms, techniques & concepts*, Jaipur, India: Historical Research Documentation Programme, 1988.

Platts, John T. *A Dictionary of Urdu, Classical Hindi and English*. 1884. Reprint, New Delhi: Oriental Books Reprint Corporation, 1977.

Rahman, R. "A tribute: Habib Rahman, 1915–1995." *Architecture+Design*, vol. xiii, no.2, March–April, 1996.

Rezavi, Syed Ali Nadeem. ""The Mighty Defensive Fort": Red Fort at Delhi Under Shahjahan–Its Plan and Structures as Described by Muhammad Waris."" *Proceedings of the Indian History Congress* 71 (2010). Accessed 30-08-2018 14:53 UTC. http://www.jstor.org/stable/44147579.

Rich, Vivian A. "Mughal Floral Painting and its European Sources." *Oriental Art*, XXXIII, no. 2 (1987).

Rizvi, Saiyid. *Fatehpur Sikri*. New Delhi: Archaeological Survey of India, 1972.

Ruggles, D. Fairchild. "Making Vision Manifest: Frame, Screen, and View in Islamic Culture." In *Sites Unseen: Landscape and Vision*, edited by Dianne Harris and D. Fairchild Ruggles. Pittsburgh PA: University of Pittsburgh Press, 2007. JSTOR, www.jstor.org/stable/j.ctt7zw9w9.11.

Saba, Matthew, curator. 'Pattern, Color, Light: Architectural Ornament in the Near East (500-1000),' Kevorkian Special Exhibitions Gallery, The Metropolitan Museum of Art, July 20, 2015–January 10, 2016. https://www.metmuseum.org/exhibitions/ listings/2015/pattern-color-light.

Sharma, Jyoti P. "A Cross-cultural Dialogue: A Case Study of Pre-Mughal Mosques in Delhi." *Built Environment* 28, no. 3 (2002). Accessed April 1, 2020. www.jstor.org/stable/23288455.

Shokoohy, M. and Shokoohy, N.H. "The Architecture of Baha Al-Din Tughrul in the Region of Bayana, Rajasthan." *Muqarnas* 4 (1987). Accessed March 25, 2020. doi:10.2307/1523099.

Skelton, Robert. "A Decorative Motif in Mughal Art". In P. Pal (ed.), *Aspects of Indian Art: Papers presented in a Symposium of the Los Angeles County Museum of Art, October 1970*, Leiden: E. J. Brill, 1972.

Smith, Edmund, W. *The Moghul Architecture of Fatehpur-Sikri: Described and illustrated by Edmund W. Smith*. Allahabad: Supdt. Govt. press, 1894–1898.

Snyder, M. "The unexpectedly tropical history of Brutalism." *The New York Times Magazine*, August 15, 2019. https://www.nytimes.com/2019/08/15/t-magazine/tropical-brutalism.html.

Stone, Nicholas. *Symbol of Divine Light: The Lamp in Islamic Culture and Other Tradition, Sacred Art in Tradition*. Bloomington, Indiana: World Wisdom, 2018.

Stronge, S. "By the Light of the Sun of Jahangir", in Bloom, Jonathan and Sheila Blair, eds. *God is the Light of the Heavens and the Earth: Light in Islamic Art and Culture*, The Biennial Hamad bin Khalifa Symposium on Islamic Art. London: Yale University Press, in association with Qatar Foundation, Virginia Commonwealth University, and Virginia Commonwealth University School of the Arts in Qatar, 2015

Thackston, W. "Light in Persian Poetry." In *God is the Light of the Heavens and the Earth: Light in Islamic Art and Culture* by Jonathan Bloom and Sheila Blair. New Haven: Yale University Press, in association with Qatar Foundation, Virginia Commonwealth University, and Virginia Commonwealth University School of the Arts in Qatar, 2015.

Thackston, Wheeler M., ed. and trans. *The Jahangirnama: Memoirs of Jahangir, Emperor of India*. New York: Freer Gallery of Art, Arthur M. Sackler Gallery in association with Oxford University Press, 1999.

Tillotson, G. "George S.T. Harris: An architect in Gwalior." *South Asian Studies*, vol. 2, 2004, pp. 13-14.

Tillotson, G. "Review of The Indian Temple Traceries by M. A. Dhaky." *Journal of the Royal Asiatic Society* 15(3) (2005). doi:10.1017/S1356186305295561.

Wade, Bonnie C. *Imaging Sound: An Ethnomusicological Study of Music, Art, and Culture in Mughal India*. Chicago: University of Chicago Press, 1998.

Welch, Anthony. "The Emperor's Grief: Two Mughal Tombs." *Muqarnas* 25 (2008). Accessed April 21, 2020. www.jstor.org/stable/27811124.

Welch, Stuart C. *India: Art and Culture*. Munich and Ahmedabad: Prestel Verlag and Mapin Publishing, 1985.

Williams, Caroline. "John Frederick Lewis: 'Reflections of Reality'." *Muqarnas* 18 (2001). Accessed April 2, 2020. doi:10.2307/1523309.

Yazdani, G. *Mandu: City of Joy*. Oxford: University Press, 1929.

Other Sources

https://archnet.org/sites/2657:

https://ghazni.bradypus.net/islamictransennas

The David Wade Archive, https://patterninislamicart. com

The Creswell Archive, https://archnet.org/ collections/12.

India International Centre, https://iicdelhi.in/history

Pair of Minbar Doors, c. 1325–30, Gallery 450, Accession Number: 91.1.2064, The Metropolitan Museum of Art, New York.

Tate Museum website: https://www.tate.org.uk/art/ artists/mona-hatoum-2365/who-is-mona-hatoum.

'Nur: Light in Art and Science from the Islamic World,' travelling exhibition, Fundacion Focus-Abengoa, Seville, Spain, October 14, 2013–February 9, 2014 and Dallas Museum of Art, Dallas, Texas, March 30, 2014–June 29, 2014.

"The Aga Khan Museum / Maki and Associates," in *ArchDaily*, 30 Jul 2018. Accessed 26 Nov 2021. https://www.archdaily.com/899013/the-aga-khanmuseum-maki-and-associates ISSN 0719-8884.

Rewal, Manu. *Indian Modernity*, https://vimeopro. com/user30788261/hall-of-nation.

Index

Image Credits

Anila Qayyum Agha: p. 253

Al Sabah Collection, Kuwait: p. 51 (fig. 17)

The Al Thani Collection 2013: p. 259

Alamy Stock Photo: pp. 66 (fig. 29), 77 (fig. 4), 108, 176, 209, 212–213, 223, 240, 248

American Institute of Indian Studies: p. 37

Ahmad Angawi: p. 257 (fig. 21)

Arthur M. Sackler Gallery: pp. 107, 208 (fig. 4)

Arts of Hindostan, Hong Kong: p. 243 (figs 4, 5)

British Library: p. 90

Qamoos Bukhari: p. 93

Cleveland Museum of Art: p. 208 (fig. 3)

Tarik Currimbhoy: p. 255 (fig. 19)

The David Collection, Copenhagen: p. 15 (fig. 4)

Dinodia Photo Library: pp. 67, 69 (fig. 34), 88 (fig. 14), 197 (fig. 12), 242 (fig. 1), 246–247 (fig. 9)

Doris Duke Foundation for Islamic Art, Honolulu, Hawaii (Photo: David Franzen, 2020): pp. 226, 228, 230, 231

Dreamstime: pp. 77 (fig. 5), 83, 88 (fig. 16), 84, 187 (fig. 15), 198, 210, 220 (fig. 18), 247 (fig. 10)

Johan Gollings: p. 195 (fig. 5)

Abhinav Goswami: Front cover, pp. 2, 6–7, 38, 42–43, 44, 45, 46, 47 (figs 9, 10), 50, 52–53, 53, 54–55 (second–fourth row), 56–57, 59, 60–61, 62–63, 64, 64–65, 66 (fig. 30), 87, 94, 96 (fig. 1), 106, 110, 111, 112, 113 (fig. 17), 114–115, 116–117, 118–119, 120–121, 122, 123, 124, 126–127, 128, 129, 130–131, 132–133, 134, 142, 150–151, 152–153, 156–157, 158–159, 161, 162–163, 166–167, 174–175, 177, 179, 180–181, 183, 184–185, 186, 204, 207, 214, 215, 216–217, 217, 218–219, 234–235, 236, 238–239, back cover

Alyn Griffiths, dezeen.com: p. 247

Navina Haidar: pp. 69 (fig. 33), 197 (fig. 11)

Zarina Hashmi: p. 257 (fig. 22)

Susan Hefuna: p. 256

David Horsman: pp. 224–225

James Ivory: p. 260

The Italian Archaeological Mission in Afghanistan: p. 82

Islamic Arts Museum Malaysia: p. 79

iStock: pp. 92, 195 (fig. 6)

Pramod Kumar KG, Eka Archiving Services Pvl. Ltd.: p. 211 (fig. 7)

Ebba Koch: pp. 136, 140, 144–145

Amir B. Jahanbin: p. 125 (figs 26a, 26b)

Shinkenchiku-sha: p. 249

The Metropolitan Museum of Art: Front endpapers, pp. 8, 14, 15 (fig. 3), 16, 17, 47 (fig. 8), 51 (fig. 16), 68, 77 (fig. 3), 96 (fig. 2), 109, 125 (fig. 27), 148 (fig. 3), 160, 195 (fig. 7), 196 (figs 9, 10), 237, 252, 258, back endpapers

George Michell: p. 30

Museo Arqueologico Provincial de Cordoba: p. 76

Amit Pasricha: pp. 192–193, 194, 211 (fig. 8)

Anand Patel: pp. 26–27, 40, 49, 54–55 (first row)

Andrea Pickl: p. 254

Private collection, New York: p. 125

Private collection, New York: p. 146

Private collection, Mumbai: p. 164

Private collection, Philadelphia: p. 203

Private collection, Mumbai: p. 206

Ram Rahman: pp. 48, 222, 242 (fig. 2),

243 (fig. 3), 245

Nimish Singh: p. 91

Sanjit Singh: pp. 74, 80–81, 84–85, 86, 98–99, 101, 102–103, 104, 105, 148–149, 168, 169, 170, 171

Upendra Sinha: pp. 70–71

Kevin Standage (https://kevinstandagephotography.wordpress.com/): p. 220 (fig. 19)

Surendra Kumar Suri: pp. 18, 20–21, 22, 24, 25, 28, 29, 32, 33, 34–35, 188, 190, 199, 199, 200, 201, 202

Shutterstock: pp. 72, 246 (fig. 8)

Tate Museum: p. 251

Giles Tillotson: p. 221

Eugenia Burnett Tinsley: pp. 146, 191

Victoria and Albert Museum, London: pp. 36, 196 (fig. 8)

Thomas Welch, Stuart Cary Welch: pp. 154–155, 173, 232

Wikimedia Commons: p. 113 (fig. 16)

Yale Center for British Art, New Haven: p. 78

Hector Zamora: p. 255 (fig. 18)

Index of Paintings and Drawings

Acknowledgements

Warm thanks are expressed to all those who have made invaluable contributions towards envisioning and realizing this publication.

We are deeply grateful for the generous support of Thomas Cary Welch, the Welch family and the Chatterjee Charitable Foundation. Their faith in the book and enthusiasm for the material have been vital to the project.

Mitchell Abdul Karim Crites's unrivalled knowledge of *jali*s, craftsmanship and craftspeople, mentorship and creativity have been essential for the making of this book. Much gratitude is expressed to George Michell and Ebba Koch for their scholarly contributions and the wealth of knowledge they have brought to the project.

The photography of *jali*s and their particular qualities is surely one of the greater challenges for the camera. This volume showcases the talents and generosity of many photographers who have demonstrated their excellence in their craft, most especially Abhinav Goswamy who captured sites, light and space over several photographic journeys. We are immensely grateful to Ram Rahman, Sanjit Singh, Surinder Kumar, Karam Puri, Amit Pasricha, Amir B. Jahanbin, Nirdesh Singh, Upendra Sinha, Anand Patel, Kevin Standage, John Gollings, David Horsman and the late Robyn Beeche for their wonderful images.

It has been a privilege to work with Mapin Publishing, whose professionalism and collegiality have made this book-making a memorable experience. Special thanks and appreciation to Bipin Shah for his wise guidance throughout. Neha Manke and Gopal Limbad have been a wonderful editorial and design team, as have other Mapin colleagues, including Rakesh Manger in the Art department.

Many scholars, writers, travellers, explorers and individuals have generously contributed ideas and perspectives. They include: Giles Tillotson, Naman Ahuja, Rana Safvi, Nilou Crites, Finbarr Barry Flood, Sue Stronge, Catherine Asher, Hasan Uddin Khan, Thalia Kennedy, and Sage Mehta. In New York thanks go to: Salman Rushdie, Amita Chatterjee, Aroon Shivdesani, Sundaram Tagore, Kiran Desai, James Ivory, Fatima Qureishi and Narmeen Husain. In Hyderabad: Uzra Bilgrami and Farzanaji. In Kashmir: Qamoos Bukhari and Hakim Asaf Ali. In Mumbai: Tasneem Zakaria Mehta, Bharatbala Ganapaty and Lynette D'mello. In Lahore: FS Aijazuddin. In Delhi: William Dalrymple, Pramod Kumar, Asaf Ali, Jenny Housego, Momin Latif, Caroline Desouza, Tulika Kedia, Shikha Jain,

Ratish Nanda and Puneetinder Kaur Sidhu. Special thanks to Nirad Grover, whose experienced eye for architecture, landscape, and bookmaking has been most valuable to the planning of this volume.

Several collectors, curators and art dealers have generously shared their treasures and perspectives. They include: Sheikha Hussa Sabah al-Salem al-Sabah, Salam Kaoukji, Seran and Ravi Trehan, Sheikh Hamad bin Abdullah Al-Thani, Amin Jaffer, Shailender Hemchand, Syed Muhammad Al-Bukhary, Amit Ambalal, Steven Kossak, John and Betty Sequeira, Judy Brick Freeman, Gursharan Sidhu, Sundaram Tagore, Thomas Welch and the Welch family, Kjeld von Folsach and the David Collection, Francesca Galloway, Antony Peattie and Terence McInerney.

Modern and contemporary artists, architects and designers have been an inspiring part of the *jali* story. Warm thanks are expressed to: James Worth, Nevin Aladag, Ahmad Angawi, Susan Hefuna, Mona Hatoum, Afruz Amighi, Hector Zamora, Anila Qayyum Agha, Waseem Ahmad, Babi Sonwani, Tarik Currimbhoy, Manu Rewal, Raj Rewal, Hala Warde, Laurie Anderson, Tarun Tahiliani and the late Zarina Hashmi and Ashok Dhawan.

Former and current Metropolitan Museum colleagues have lent generous support: Martina Rugiadi, Maryam Ekhtiar, Deniz Beyazit, Courtney Stewart, Annick Des Roches, Shane Morrissey, Helen Goldenberg, Ria Breed, Nadine Orenstein, Kim Benzel, Sean Hemingway, Iria Candela, Abraham Thomas, Sophia Geronimus, Sheila Canby, Andrea Bayer, Max Hollein, Philippe de Montebello, the Department of Asian Art, Anna Marie Kellen and the Photograph Studio.

For special images, we thank Leslee Michelson and Kristen Remington of The Shangri La Museum of Islamic Art, Culture and Design, Honolulu; the American Institute of Indian Studies, Varanasi; Michael Chagnon and Bita Pourvash of the Aga Khan Museum, Toronto; Debra Diamond of the Smithsonian's National Museum of Asian Art; Sunanya Rathore of the Mehrangarh Museum Trust; Elizabeth Marano; and Anjali Kothari.

Friends and family have been on the *jali* journey for a long time and their support and enthusiasm has meant the world.

Navina Najat Haidar